GOD
AND
GOVERNMENT
BREAKING THE MYTH OF SEPARATION AND THE DEEPENING EVANGELICAL DIVISION IN AMERICAN POLITICS

Published by Dominion Life, Inc.
Chicago, USA.

ALSO BY JOSHUA M NGOMA:

Prophets, Miracles, and the "Prosperity Gospel"
The Africans: A Continent on the rise
True Worshipers

GOD
AND
GOVERNMENT

BREAKING THE MYTH OF SEPARATION AND THE DEEPENING EVANGELICAL DIVISION IN AMERICAN POLITICS

Joshua Ngoma

In Honor of Dad

MYSRIP

Table of Contents

Introduction

In a most general sense, Evangelicals believe in the absolute authority of the Bible as the word of God, in salvation through Jesus Christ, and in the need to spread the gospel to the utter most parts of the earth.

The Evangelical Church in the United States and in many other parts of the world, in general, is in a crisis of identity. It is stuck at a pivotal crossroads of history, conflicted about its role and direction.

This status quo of paralysis has been magnified by a renewed and raging debate about the role of Christianity in public affairs and the destiny of nations.

There is also a growing and deepening divide within the Evangelical movement itself, between the so-called Religious Right and the Religious Left, concerning which direction the country's politics ought to take.

The religious right, also known as the Christian right, are conservative Christians whose political views are characterized by their strong support of socially conservative policies.

The religious left or the Christian left believes in

9

social justice and aligns with social movements that care for the impoverished and oppressed groups.

This debate was intensified during the Obama administration with the U.S. Supreme Court ruling in April of 2015, that states must legalize same-sex marriage, igniting the long existing battle between the "Separation of Church and State" over the issue.

Epitomizing this debate, were comments made by Bishop TD Jakes during an interview with the Huffington Post about the role of the Church in American politics.

The interview ignited a "firestorm" response on social media and other news outlets from different sections of Christendom.

 I have used Bishop Jakes' interview, and similar public discussions from other prominent church leaders, only for purposes of highlighting the crises issues that have deepened the division within the Church in America with regards to its role and responsibilities in the public affairs of the nation.

I have attempted to deal with each assumption by giving a Biblical and historical perspective.

Bishop Jakes advocated for the separation of Church and State, which would allow for "all types of people" to have whatever rights they desire despite Biblical prohibitions. He said that politics don't need to be based on Christianity.

Bishop TD Jakes is a prominent Church leader in Evangelical circles and a prominent trailblazer in the Charismatic movement.

He is the Bishop at the Potters House in Dallas Texas in the United States.

Here is the transcript of Bishop TD Jake's interview:

"[O]nce you get past [thinking America is a Christian nation] … Once you begin to understand that democracy—that a republic actually—is designed to be an overarching system to protect our unique nuances, then we no longer look for public policy to reflect biblical ethics," Bishop Jakes explained.

"If we can divide—or what you would call separation of Church and State—then we can dwell together more effectively because atheists, agnostics, Jews, all types of people, Muslims, pay into the government.

The government then cannot reflect one particular view over another just because we're the dominant group of religious people in [this] country because those numbers are changing every day," he asserted. "We need a neutralized government that protects our right to disagree with one another and agree with one another."

During the same interview, a viewer asked Bishop Jakes if he believes that homosexuals and the black church can co-exist.

"Absolutely," he replied. "An obvious yes; the Church ain't turning nobody away," Marc Lamont Hill, the interviewer added, "How should the black church and the LGBT community co-exist?"

Bishop Jakes replied, "I think it is going to be diverse from church to church. Every church has a different opinion on the issue and every gay person is different,"

"And I think that to speak that the church—the black church, the white church or any kind of church you wanna call it—are all the same, is totally not true."

Bishop Jakes further added that he thinks homosexuals should find congregations that affirm their lifestyle.

"LGBT's of different types and sorts have to find a place of worship that reflects what your views are and what you believe like anyone else," he outlined.

"The church should have the right to have its own convictions and values; if you don't like those convictions and values [and] you totally disagree with it, don't try to change my house, move into your own … and find somebody who gets what you get about faith," Jakes added.

12

When asked if his thinking has "evolved," Jakes agreed that it has.

"Evolved and evolving," he replied. When asked how, Jakes said, "I think that where I am is to better understand we, the church, bought into the myth that this is a Christian nation."

"That's outside the Church," Hill remarked. "Inside the Church, has your thinking shifted biblically, Scripturally, hermeneutically at all? The reason I ask that is because I talk to a lot of ministers now …. and one of the questions [at a recent African meeting] was, is there a way to approach Christian tradition—Christian Scripture—in light of a new understanding of LGBT?"

Hill then pointed to the issue of slavery, and that "irrespective of what [biblical] text says literally, we don't support slavery as a body." He asked if there was likewise "room for that same kind of shift" when it comes to homosexuality.

Jakes said that he believed that the shift needed to occur "behind the closed doors of the church" to avoid being called names by society for disagreeing on the matter. He added moments later that the issue of homosexuality is "complex."

"Paul spends a lot of time wrestling back and forth, trying to understand should a woman wear a head covering, should you cut your hair," Jakes stated. "I

13

mean, they grappled back then and we're grappling now because we're humans and we are flawed and we're not God."

"Once you understand you're not God, you leave yourself an 'out' clause to grow," he said.

Bishop Jakes clarified his stance on his Facebook page following the backlash. He expressed outrage remarking that he was "shocked" at how his comments were misinterpreted.

He reiterated that while he personally disagrees with homosexual "marriage," he, however, respects the government's provision of it.

"My comment on HuffPo TV drifted into issues of the Supreme Court ruling and changing the world through public policy versus personal witness.

Further, I have come to respect that I can't force my beliefs on others by controlling public policy for taxpayers [sic] and other U.S. citizens," he wrote.

"Jesus never sought to change the world through public policy but rather through personal transformation. All people didn't embrace him either," Jakes continued. "That's what I said and what I meant …. Nothing more and nothing less."

He explained that when he used the phrase "evolved and evolving" in response to interviewer Marc Lamont Hill's question, he was only referring

14

to the methods used to minister to homosexuals, not his position on the issue.

"When asked about the 'black church' and its role in ministering to gay people, I briefly mentioned (we were running out of time the word 'evolved and evolving' regarding my approach over the 39 years of my ministry to gay people who choose to come to our services," Jakes wrote. "I simply meant that my method is evolving—not my message."

"I was shocked to read that this was manipulated in a subsequent article to say I endorsed same-sex marriage! My position on the subject has been steadfast and rooted in Scripture," he continued.

Jakes concluded by stating that although he personally opposes same-sex "marriage," he "respects the rights" given to homosexuals by the U.S. government—as he had outlined during the Huffington Post interview.

"For the record, I do not endorse same-sex marriage but I respect the rights that this country affords those that disagree with me," he remarked. (End of transcript

From this interview by Bishop TD Jakes, and the fiery debates that ensued among many believers, I derived the following presumptions:

1. Can the Church look to public policy to reflect Biblical ethics?

15

2. Should the Government reflect one particular religious view over another?

3. Did Jesus seek to change the world through public policy or rather through personal transformation?

4. Can the Church change the world through public policy or by personal witness alone?

5. Should Christian believers force their beliefs on others by controlling public policy for taxpayers?

6. Should the Government make provision and exercise neutrality for all people to live as they wish as long as they also pay taxes?

7. Was the United States of America founded as a Christian nation?

8. What is God's Kingdom on earth?

9. What is the "Separation of Church and State"?

10. What does the Bible teach about Government and the role of the Church in politics?

For unto us a Child is born,
Unto us a Son is given;
And the **government** will be upon His shoulder.
And His name will be called
Wonderful, Counselor, Mighty God,
Everlasting Father, Prince of Peace.
Of the increase of *His* government and peace
There will be no end,
Upon the throne of David and over His kingdom,
To order it and establish it with judgment and justice
From that time forward, even forever.
The zeal of the LORD of hosts will perform this.

Isaiah 9:6-7

CHAPTER 1

WHAT IS GOD'S KINGDOM ON EARTH?

The Kingdom of God's origins are from the Heavens and extend in all the earth.

Even in the "Lord's prayer", we are impressed to call "God's will and His Kingdom to come here on earth as it is in heaven".

After Jesus Christ's Resurrection, He declared:

[8]All authority has been given to Me in heaven and on earth. [19]Go therefore and make disciples of all the nations, baptizing them in the name of the Father and of the Son and of the Holy Spirit, [20]teaching them to observe all things that I have commanded you; and lo, I am with you always, *even* to the end of the age. Amen. Matthew 28: 18-20

From the the Bible's great commission of Matthew chapter 28 it is established that:

1. Christ is Sovereign over heaven and earth but ever present with His people.

2. He is a supreme commander of a hierarchy and has delegated authority to His followers to bring the nations under Christ's authority.

3. His Kingdom is that of law and ethics.

4. His followers, the Christians, are commanded to teach or disciple men, women, and children to observe and obey all that He commands.

5. His followers are instructed to disciple the nations for Christ and to announce Him as ruler of the nations.

6. He judges the nations.

7. His Kingdom is in perpetuity, passed on from one generation of believers to the next.

8. He promises to be with His people until the end of time.

Jesus proclaimed that His kingdom will stand but the Kingdoms of this world, and Satan's will utterly fall.

The kingdoms of this world have become *the kingdoms* of our Lord and of His Christ, and He shall reign forever and ever! Rev 11:15
Nation by nation and Satan's inherently divided Kingdom will fall to Christ and not the other way round.

The kingdom of God is not of this world.

[36] Jesus answered, "My kingdom is not of this world. If My kingdom were of this world, My servants would fight, so that I should not be delivered to the Jews; but now My kingdom is not from here. John 18:36

But Jesus did not say His kingdom does not operate in this world. He also did not say His Kingdom does not operate over this world.

He simply was emphasizing the origin of His Kingdom, power, and authority.

For example, Caiphas the High Priest interrogated Jesus on religious questions. He was concerned with establishing whether or not Jesus claimed to be "the Christ, the Son of God". `

[57] And those who had laid hold of Jesus led *Him* away to Caiaphas the high priest, where the scribes and the elders were assembled.
[58] But Peter followed Him at a distance to the high priest's courtyard. And he went in and sat with the servants to see the end.

[59]Now the chief priests, the elders, and all the council sought false testimony against Jesus to put Him to death, [60] but found none. Even though many false witnesses came forward, they found none. But at last two false witnesses came forward

[61] and said, "This *fellow* said, 'I am able to destroy the temple of God and to build it in three days.'" [62] And the high priest arose and said to Him, "Do You answer nothing? What is it these men testify against You?" But Jesus kept silent.

And the high priest answered and said to Him, "I put You under oath by the living God: Tell us if You are the Christ, the Son of God!"64 Jesus said to him, "It is as you said. Nevertheless, I say to you, hereafter you will see the Son of Man sitting at the right hand of the Power, and coming on the clouds of heaven."
Matthew 26:57-64

But the religious argument did not concern Pilate. Pilate's concern was to establish whether or not Jesus had posed a political threat to his Jurisdiction or that of Rome.

The accusers of Jesus fabricated these charges in order to bring Jesus before Pilate.

[2] And they began to accuse Him, saying, "We found this *fellow* perverting the nation, and forbidding to pay taxes to Caesar, saying that He Himself is Christ, a King.
Luke 23:2

The Kingdom of God cannot be brought about on earth politically through civil governments but through regeneration by the finished work of Jesus Christ on the cross.

In turn, regenerated men and women will affect and change every walk of life including politics.

[21]nor will they say, 'See here!' or 'See there!' For

indeed, the kingdom of God is within you." Luke 17:21

21

God is sovereign over His Kingdom and He reigns with justice and perfect knowledge.

As humans, we are His responsible agents on earth.

His Kingdom is likened to leaven, steadily growing and replacing the divided Kingdoms of the Devil.

The kingdom of heaven is like leaven, which a woman took and hid in three measures of meal till it was all leavened. Matthew 13:3

[9] A little leaven leavens the whole lump. Galatians 5:9

To redeem the world does not necessarily mean that the world will be made perfect.

Just like we were dead in sin, Christ redeemed us but we are not perfect.

Judicially, as sinners, we stand before God as perfect because we have the perfection and righteousness of Christ imputed to us.

We have not been made righteous, we have been declared righteous.

[21] But now apart from the law the righteousness of God has been made known, to which the Law and the Prophets testify. [22] This righteousness is given through faith in Jesus Christ to all who believe. There is no difference between Jew and Gentile, [23] for all have sinned and fall short of the glory of God, [24] and all are justified freely by his grace through the redemption that came by Christ Jesus. [25] God presented Christ as a sacrifice of atonement, through the shedding of his

blood—to be received by faith. He did this to
demonstrate his righteousness, because in his
forbearance he had left the sins committed beforehand
unpunished— [26] he did it to demonstrate his
righteousness at the present time, so as to be just and the
one who justifies those who have faith in Jesus. Romans
3:21-26, NIV

[13] He has delivered us from the power of darkness and
conveyed *us* into the kingdom of the Son of His love,
[14] in whom we have redemption through His blood, the
forgiveness of sins. Colossians 1:13-14

[13] Christ has redeemed us from the curse of the law,
having become a curse for us (for it is written, "Cursed
is everyone who hangs on a tree"). Galatians 3:13

[17] for the kingdom of God is not eating and drinking, but
righteousness and peace and joy in the Holy Spirit.
Romans 14:17

Through sanctification, we are required to conform
our lives more and more in the image of Jesus
Christ and the effects of our sin nature will finally
be eradicated when we are raised as imperishable.

[42] So also *is* the resurrection of the dead. *The body* is
sown in corruption, it is raised in incorruption. 1
Corinthians 15:42

The redeemed Christian is the agent of change as
the salt and light here on earth.

Over time, only self-governed people under the rule
of God's word can sustain the growth of God's
Kingdom.

Even in the Ten Commandments (Exodus 20:1-20), the first five deals with what man owes to God and the last five deals with what man owes to his fellow man.

Wherever the gospel has changed individuals, it has changed civilizations, in turn, and the advance of secularism is the direct result of the Church's retreat.

During Jesus' ministry and the early Church, there was heightened demonic activity and opposition but it was not the mark of the end of the world. It was just the beginning of the Church age. (Acts 17:6)

Similarly, Christians should not resign to the heightened demonic activity of our time to mean that the world is "soon" coming to an end.

As it gets spiritually darker in the world, it ought to get brighter and more distinct in the Church.

Arise, shine;
For your light has come!
And the glory of the LORD is risen upon you.
[2] For behold, the darkness shall cover the earth,
And deep darkness the people;
But the LORD will arise over you,
And His glory will be seen upon you. Isaiah 60:1-2

We have overcome because of the Christ in us, the hope of glory!

[4] You are of God, little children, and have overcome them, because He who is in you is greater than he who is in the world. 1 John 4:4

God has more power than the Devil. Satan has power but God limits it.

During Jesus' earthly ministry, the disciples had authority and power over demons.

But whatever city you enter, and they do not receive you, go out into its streets and say, 'The very dust of your city which clings to us we wipe off against you. Nevertheless know this, that the kingdom of God has come near you.' 12 But I say to you that it will be more tolerable in that Day for Sodom than for that city.13 "Woe to you, Chorazin! Woe to you, Bethsaida! For if the mighty works which were done in you had been done in Tyre and Sidon, they would have repented long ago, sitting in sackcloth and ashes. 14 But it will be more tolerable for Tyre and Sidon at the judgment than for you. 15 And you, Capernaum, who are exalted to heaven, will be brought down to Hades. 16 He who hears you hears Me, he who rejects you rejects Me, and he who rejects Me rejects Him who sent Me."17 Then the seventy returned with joy, saying, "Lord, even the demons are subject to us in Your name."18 And He said to them, "I saw Satan fall like lightning from heaven. 19 Behold, I give you the authority to trample on serpents and scorpions, and over all the power of the enemy, and nothing shall by any means hurt you. 20 Nevertheless do not rejoice in this, that the spirits are subject to you, but rather rejoice because your names are written in heaven."
Luke 10: 10-20

The casting out of demons in Jesus' ministry was the sign that the Kingdom of God has come to displace the enemy territory of Satan.

As Christians, we can spoil the work of the devil because he has limited power over believers.

Satan's influence on how much he could afflict Job was restricted. (Job 1:12, 2:6)

When we stand in Christ, Satan cannot "touch" us.

[18] We know that whoever is born of God does not sin; but he who has been born of God keeps himself, and the wicked one does not touch him.1 John 5:18

His works have been destroyed.

[8] He who sins is of the devil, for the devil has sinned from the beginning. For this purpose the Son of God was manifested, that He might destroy the works of the devil. 1 John 3:8

He must flee when resisted.

[7] Therefore submit to God. Resist the devil and he will flee from you. James 4:7

He has been rendered powerless over the believers.

[14] Inasmuch then as the children have partaken of flesh and blood, He Himself likewise shared in the same, that through death He might destroy him who had the power of death, that is, the devil. Hebrews 2:14

Greater is the Christ in us, than the evil one in the world.

[4] You are of God, little children, and have overcome them, because He who is in you is greater than he who is in the world. 1 John 4:4

These scriptures are rendered useless when Christians incorrectly hold the notion that Satan is in control or that his "controlling" influence will continue.

If Christians do nothing, we can expect Satan's kingdom to advance.

Satan's power over the world remains as long as the nations are not discipled. (Matthew 28: 18-20)

Satan can only be in control of the governments of the world when Christians are irresponsible in the transformation of civil realms of power.

As believers, we have no excuse because God has disarmed the "rulers and the authorities".

[15] Having disarmed principalities and powers, He made a public spectacle of them, triumphing over them in it. Col 2:15

Through the crucifixion, the powers of darkness were brought to light. Jesus has exposed the powers of darkness and Satan's mask of deception has been ripped off of him.

[13] He has delivered us from the power of darkness and conveyed *us* into the kingdom of the Son of His love. Col 1:13

Therefore, if Satan does not have as much power as God, then the people who follow Satan cannot have as much power as the Christians who follow God.

27

We pray for the Kingdom of God to come and dwell in the hearts of men, women and children.

What we effectively pray for in the spiritual realm affects the natural realm and order of things and this is where our victories are first manifested.

[12] For we do not wrestle against flesh and blood, but against principalities, against powers, against the rulers of the darkness of this age, against spiritual *hosts* of wickedness in the heavenly *places.* [13] Therefore take up the whole armor of God, that you may be able to withstand in the evil day, and having done all, to stand. Ephesians 6:12-13

For instance, Prophet Daniel understood the seasons and times of God.

Daniel understood from reading the scriptures, according to the prophetic words given by the Prophet Jeremiah that the anguish of Jerusalem's captivity was to last for only seventy years under the Babylonian empire.

Daniel set out to petition God concerning this matter, in prayer, fasting, sackcloth, and ashes. (Daniel 9: 1-4

Daniel was among thousands of captives who were taken from Judah as exiles into Babylon between 605 B.C and 582 B.C, alongside treasures from both Solomon's palace and the temple.

The Babylonians had subdued and consolidated their rule covering an area engulfing almost the entire Middle East.

To govern such a large Kingdom, they sought help from some of their slaves who were educated and had skills to help the Babylonians govern.

Daniel was among the four Hebrews who were found to be good-looking, gifted in Wisdom, knowledge and quick to understand. The other three were Hananiah, Mishael, and Azariah. (Daniel 1:4-7)

Although Daniel's prayer was heard by God on the very first day he set out to pray, the answer did not get back to him by God's messenger until after twenty-one days. The answer was held back because of warfare in the heavenly realms.

[12] Then he said to me, "Do not fear, Daniel, for from the first day that you set your heart to understand, and to humble yourself before your God, your words were heard; and I have come because of your words. [13] But the prince of the kingdom of Persia withstood me twenty-one days; and behold, Michael, one of the chief princes, came to help me, for I had been left alone there with the kings of Persia. [14] Now I have come to make you understand what will happen to your people in the latter days, for the vision *refers* to *many* days yet *to come.* Daniel 10:12-14

Jesus also tells us that we cannot enter a home
(village, county, city or nation for that matter)
unless we bind the strong man of that home first.

 But Jesus knew their thoughts, and said to them: "Every
kingdom divided against itself is brought to desolation,
and every city or house divided against itself will not
stand. 26 If Satan casts out Satan, he is divided against
himself. How then will his kingdom stand? 27 And if I
cast out demons by Beelzebub, by whom do your sons
cast them out? Therefore they shall be your judges. 28
But if I cast out demons by the Spirit of God, surely the
kingdom of God has come upon you. 29 Or how can one
enter a strong man's house and plunder his goods, unless
he first binds the strong man? And then he will plunder
his house. Matthew 12:25-29

One of the most damaging and unbalanced
"doctrines" in the Church today is the belief that
Jesus is coming back soon using man's concept of
"soon" and that the world is headed for an
inevitable destruction.

The thinking further perpetuates this notion that
there is nothing Christians can do to stop this
inevitable slide into destruction.

*A balanced attitude ought to be; that we live
upright lives anticipating Christ's coming back at
any moment but plan for our lives, families,
Churches, and nations as if He will not return for
the next hundred years or so.*

The Church is pre-occupied and worried about trying to figure out God's timetable when she ought to be busy with the affairs of the Kingdom.

At the ascension, the disciples of Jesus asked Him if at that time He would restore the Kingdom of Israel. But Jesus directed their focus from the final restoration to the work at hand.

[6] Therefore, when they had come together, they asked Him, saying, "Lord, will You at this time restore the kingdom to Israel?" [7] And He said to them, "It is not for you to know times or seasons which the Father has put in His own authority. [8] But you shall receive power when the Holy Spirit has come upon you; and you shall be witnesses to Me in Jerusalem, and in all Judea and Samaria, and to the end of the earth. Acts 1:6-8

God requires of us to keep working regardless of external circumstances.

[4] He who observes the wind will not sow, And he who regards the clouds will not reap. Ecclesiastes 11:4

Kingdom work requires faithfulness.

[13] So he called ten of his servants, delivered to them ten minas, and said to them, 'Do business till I come.' Luke 19:13

Civilizations come and go. Great Kingdoms, Empires, and nations have come and gone.

Only the Kingdom of God goes on forever, from strength to strength, engulfing the whole earth just as the waters cover the seas.

The notion that the advance of God's Kingdom and Christian civilization will inevitably dwindle and phase away is an illusion.

Christ is building His Church here on earth and the powers of hell will not prevail. He has also given us the keys to His kingdom's authority.

[13] When Jesus came into the region of Caesarea Philippi, He asked His disciples, saying, "Who do men say that I, the Son of Man, am?" [14] So they said, "Some *say* John the Baptist, some Elijah, and others Jeremiah or one of the prophets.[15] He said to them, "But who do you say that I am?" [16] Simon Peter answered and said, "You are the Christ, the Son of the living God." [17] Jesus answered and said to him, "Blessed are you, Simon Bar-Jonah, for flesh and blood has not revealed *this* to you, but My Father who is in heaven. [18] And I also say to you that you are Peter, and on this rock I will build My church, and the gates of Hades shall not prevail against it. [19] And I will give you the keys of the kingdom of heaven, and whatever you bind on earth will be bound in heaven, and whatever you loose on earth will be loosed in heaven." Matthew 16:13-19

In the Lord's Prayer Jesus asks us to pray:

"For Yours is the kingdom and the power and the glory forever. Amen." Matthew 6:13

Kingdoms, nations, and empires built on the shaky foundation of man cannot last and will not stand the test of time. Eventually, they become dust under God's justice.

Unless the LORD builds the house,
They labor in vain who build it;
Unless the LORD guards the city,
The watchman stays awake in vain. Psalm 127:1

This was King Nebuchadnezzar's dream of the human colossus, which the prophet Daniel interpreted.

[31] "You, O king, were watching; and behold, a great image! This great image, whose splendor *was* excellent, stood before you; and its form *was* awesome. [32] This image's head *was* of fine gold, its chest and arms of silver, its belly and thighs of bronze, [33] its legs of iron, its feet partly of iron and partly of clay. [34] You watched while a stone was cut out without hands, which struck the image on its feet of iron and clay, and broke them in pieces. [35] Then the iron, the clay, the bronze, the silver, and the gold were crushed together, and became like chaff from the summer threshing floors; the wind carried them away so that no trace of them was found. And the stone that struck the image became a great mountain and filled the whole earth. Daniel 2: 31-35

The Kingdom of God is the stone cut without hands that became a mountain that filled the earth.

Jesus Christ, through His redeemed people on earth, is the fulfillment of this prophecy.

[5] you also, as living stones, are being built up a spiritual house, a holy priesthood, to offer up spiritual sacrifices acceptable to God through Jesus Christ. 1 Peter 2:5

As the body of Christ on earth, we have relegated ourselves to defeat as the only option in the face of rising Secularism.

The thinking is, if things really get real bad, God will "Rapture" us out of this mess.

The enemy has convinced a whole generation of Christians that they will have nothing to pass onto their children and grandchildren because the church will be "Raptured" out of the world before our children can inherit it.

What if Christ does not return for the next hundred to a thousand years or so?

What kind of legacy and inheritance will we leave behind for our children as Christians?

We are sitting on the sidelines of life, confined to the walls of our beautiful Sanctuaries, waiting for God to bail us out.

This is beyond just electing a Christian leader. We should instead build up spiritual capital, economic capital, educational capital and political capital and pass it on to the future generations to come.

It is our God-given task to subdue the earth to His glory through cumulative efforts of His people. It will not be accomplished in one single generation.

It can easily be depressing when you see how today's Christians are far from this truth compared to the unbelievers in various areas.

We have lost a lot of ground over the past Century or so. It will take a mass revival of these truths to recover ground much quicker. It will take time and a consented effort by the Church to get it back.

This revival will involve calling Christians to exercise greater responsibility under God than ever before.

We have to take responsibility seriously in a generation that expects results and continued benefits without sacrifice and due process.

This revival would not mean much without an army of well-trained and Biblically self-conscious professionals in every area such as Business, Law, Media, Sport, Entertainment, and politics.

Above all, we need to witness to the world about Jesus Christ and get the whole world to acknowledge Him as the King of kings and Lord of lords.

We have a huge task ahead of us but God's beginnings are always humble.

[10] For who has despised the day of small things? Zechariah 4:10

It is not where we start but where we finish that matters. We need to start from somewhere teaching and living these truths again.

The giant Goliath was not a problem for David with just a few stones in hand.

The giants in the land of Canaan were not a deterrent to Joshua and Caleb getting into the Promised Land.

Jesus says all we need to move a mountain is faith as a mustard seed.

Every time the people of God considered retreat in the face of opposition, God rebuked them for their unbelief.

When the twelve spies were sent out to Canaan, God had already promised them in advance that the land was theirs. (Numbers 13:2)

Ten came back with a report of unbelief, but Joshua and Caleb were the exceptions. There were giants in the land and Joshua and Caleb did not deny this. They figured that God had made the promise hence the land was theirs.

In the eyes of Joshua and Caleb, giants were but a minor and temporary inconvenience.

This fear of the giants and unbelief, led to the people of Israel wasting forty years wandering in the wilderness.

Forty years later, two spies were sent out to Jericho and Rahab told the real state of affairs in the camp of Israel's enemies.

[8] Before the spies lay down for the night, she went up on the roof [9] and said to them, "I know that the LORD has given you this land and that a great fear of you has fallen on us, so that all who live in this country are melting in fear because of you. We have heard how the LORD dried up the water of the Red Sea for you when you came out of Egypt, and what you did to Sihon and Og, the two kings of the Amorites east of the Jordan, whom you completely destroyed. Joshua 2:8-10, NIV

Similarly, the Secularists of today are just as frightened of the Church as the people of Jericho were the Israelites.

However, what makes the difference is that the Church, on the most part, does not know this.

God waited for that generation of unbelief to die and allowed Joshua and Caleb to lead the next generation to victory. (Numbers 14: 21-23, Joshua 15:13-19)

Only God alone is Self-determining

The source of sovereignty is the source of our freedoms. Who is sovereign in your life and to whom are you ultimately responsible?

Sovereignty resides in God and delegated to men and women through whom He administers His Kingdom here on earth.

God alone is self-determining and does not answer to anyone but everyone else is judicially accountable to Him and other people.

Our basic responsibility is to God and He is the source of our freedom.

But if sovereignty resides in the State, whether be a Monarchy or a Democracy, man has no appeal beyond the law and dictates of the State and has no other source of ethics apart from it.

Man becomes limited to and totally responsible for that order and the rights awarded to him by the State.

Therefore, if a man is a creation of the State or merely a "social being", then he needs to be understood in the context of the State and he cannot live or aspire beyond the political order.

As Christians, we are created in the image and likeness of God and cannot be contained in anything short of God's eternal ruling and order of things.

[27] So God created man in His *own* image; in the image of God He created him; male and female He created them.
Genesis 1:27

As Christians, we understand man in the context of God Himself.

God is the only true sovereign while other rulers are delegated sovereigns.

[5] 'I have made the earth, the man and the beast that *are* on the ground, by My great power and by My outstretched arm, and have given it to whom it seemed proper to Me.
Jeremiah 27:5

[15] By me kings reign, and rulers decree justice.

Proverbs 8:15

CHAPTER 2

THE SHIFT IN RELIGIOUS FREEDOMS IN THE OBAMA ERA

Many Evangelical Christians' contentions with the Obama administration was founded on the notion that it had shifted in guaranteeing constitutional religious freedoms by overreaching its role in the Church's institutions and functions.

The overwhelming Evangelical support for candidate Trump in the 2016 presidential elections was, in part, a backlash on the Obama administration's assault on long held religious freedoms and traditions in the United States.

Candidate Trump's campaign platform promised the restoration of these religious freedoms.

The contentious shift in these religious freedoms ranged from the re-definition of marriage to include same-sex marriage to interference in the internal affairs of religious groups and in the selection of their leaders.

Faith-based groups and organizations were mandated to provide contraceptives, sterilization services, and abortion-inducing drugs such as the morning- after contraceptive pill to their employees.

Perhaps the biggest controversy was the re-definition of traditional marriage between one man and one woman, to include same-sex couples.

Christians consider the family, as defined in the Bible, as the second layer in God's structure of Government, namely; the individual, family, Church, and State.

Further, the dispute by many Christians is that under the new same-sex marriage law, they are now compelled to offer business such as wedding related services, to same-sex couples against their religious beliefs.

The Obama administration also issued guidelines to all public schools nationwide, to allow transgender students to use bathrooms matching gender identity and not their sex at birth.

In April of 2016, the Republican Governor of the state of Mississippi, Gov. Phil Bryant, signed into law a measure that protects such religious freedoms:

"The new law states that it protects "sincerely held religious beliefs or moral convictions," including the belief that marriage is only between a man and a woman and that sexual relations should only occur in such a marriage. It also says that a person's gender is "determined by anatomy and genetics at time of birth"and goes on to say that businesses can determine who is allowed to access bathrooms, dressing rooms and locker rooms."

The states of North Carolina and Georgia have also attempted to pass similar laws.

The Obama administration's new guidelines on bathroom use for transgender students were based on the interpretation of the education department's Title IX, which states that "[n]o person in the United States shall, on the basis of sex, be excluded from participation in, be denied the benefits of, or be subjected to discrimination under any education program or activity receiving Federal financial assistance."

Consequently, 51 families in the state of Illinois sued against the US Departments of Justice and Education for pressuring District 211 with the loss of $6 million in federal funding if it did not allow a transgender "female" to use the girls' bathroom.

The lawsuit argued that there is nothing in Title IX and its regulations that use the term "gender identity" that described the type of discrimination prohibited.

The phrase "gender identity" does not appear in the text of Title IX and its regulations. The use of the term "sex" in Title IX means male or female "under the traditional conception of sex consistent with one's birth or biological sex".

Same-Sex Marriage

It was a milestone development when President Barack Obama gave a public approval of same-sex marriage in May of 2012.

The disagreement by many Christians against same-sex marriage is based on the central teaching on marriage by Jesus Christ in Matthew 19:4-6:

 And He answered and said to them, "Have you not read that He who made them at the beginning 'made them male and female,' 5 and said, 'For this reason a man shall leave his father and mother and be joined to his wife, and the two shall become one flesh'? 6 So then, they are no longer two but one flesh. Therefore what God has joined together, let not man separate."

Christians and other faith-based groups can genuinely uphold this teaching without becoming disagreeable or homophobic, but with understanding, that those who practice or advocate for same-sex marriage are also members of our own families, communities, schoolmates, workmates and church members.

So when you, a mere human being, pass judgment on them and yet do the same things, do you think you will escape God's judgment? 4 Or do you show contempt for the riches of his kindness, forbearance and patience, not realizing that God's kindness is intended to lead you to repentance? Romans 2:3-4,NIV

The United States Supreme Court ruled to re-define what constitutes marriage to now include same-sex couples.

Consequently, there is now increased public advocacy for LGBTQ rights across the world.

This announcement by the Obama administration gave impetus to the efforts of Evangelical Republicans to vote for Romney in the 2012 presidential elections because of his stance against gay marriage. The backlash was also visible among African American Evangelical Christians, even among those with Democratic leanings.
But the National Association for the Advancement of Colored People (NAACP), the oldest black civil rights organization, board of directors passed a resolution expressing support for same-sex marriage equality.

The NAACP's board voted at a leadership retreat in Miami, Florida to back a resolution supporting marriage equality.

The premise was based on the mission of the civil rights organization, which reads "The mission of the NAACP has always been to ensure the political, social and economic equality of all people" and that "We have and will oppose efforts to codify discrimination into law."

The organization's platform on marriage equality further states that, "Civil marriage is a civil right and a matter of civil law. The NAACP's support for marriage equality is deeply rooted in the Fourteenth

Amendment of the United States Constitution and equal protection of all people.

The NAACP had initially criticized North Carolina's Amendment 1, which passed in a referendum earlier in May 2012 and defined marriage as a union between "man and woman."

But a coalition of black churches denounced the NAACP endorsement of same-sex marriage.

The National Black Church Initiative, a faith-based coalition of 34,000 African American and Latino churches comprised of 15 denominations, opposed president Obama and the NAACP's endorsements of same-sex marriage.

The coalition warned that President Obama and the NAACP would lose support among black churches for their stand.

"We love our gay brothers and sisters, but the black church will never support gay marriage," and "It is and always will be against the ethics and teaching of our Lord Jesus Christ."

A number of minorities who voted for President Obama in 2008 found it difficult to support him in 2012 because they could not reconcile his stance on same-sex marriage with their Christian faith.

They felt offended by those who would compare the fight for "marriage equality" with their centuries-long struggle for civil rights by black people.

 Their argument was that there is no ambiguity in the struggle to end Slavery and Jim Crow from the Scriptures.

Beyond the theological objection to same-sex marriage, some Evangelicals see societal problems as a consequence of attempts to re-define marriage in the country.

They have cited studies that demonstrate that depression, incarceration, and even suicide are more prevalent among children who are not reared in families of married heterosexual couples.

But the proponents of same-sex marriage disagree. They have also quoted the research results to the contrary.

The American Academy of Pediatrics says, "Scientific literature demonstrates that same-sex couples' children fare as well."

The American Psychiatric Association says, "Research indicates that optimal development for children is based not on the sexual orientation of the parents."

Windsor V. The United States

Prior to being ruled unconstitutional, the Defense of Marriage Act (DOMA, was the United States federal law that defined marriage for federal purposes as the union of one man and one woman, and allowed States to refuse the recognition of same-sex marriages granted under the laws of other States.

DOMA was enacted by the 104th Congress in 1996 and signed into law by President Bill Clinton.

Its purpose was to define and protect the institution of marriage.

In a landmark ruling of 5 to 4, the US Supreme Court struck down section 3 of DOMA, which prevented the federal government from recognizing same-sex marriages citing that it violated the Constitution's "equal protection" promise.

This was in a case led by Edith Windsor against the United States after she was forced to pay in excess of $360,000 in estate taxes after her same-sex spouse died. The federal government did not recognize her marriage.

Edith Windsor and Thea Spyer was a couple and lived together in New York City for 44 years and were finally married in Canada in May 2007.

Two years later, Thea passed away. She had lived for decades with multiple sclerosis, which led to progressive paralysis.

The federal government refused to recognize their marriage and taxed Edith's inheritance from Thea.

As a result of this ruling, the US Supreme Court found DOMA to be unconstitutional and same-sex marriage was federally recognized.

However, section 2 of DOMA was not repealed. The individual States are still not required to legalize or recognize a lawful marriage from another State.

The Supreme Court ruling on DOMA has effected major changes on families regarding different federal rights attached to marital benefits.

Same-sex married couples now have joint income tax filing and exemption from federal estate taxes, social security benefits for widows and widowers, political contribution laws, Rights to creative and intellectual property, hospital visitation rights and health care benefits.

In the military, the benefits will include military health insurance, increased base and housing allowances, relocation allowance and surviving spousal benefits and internment at Arlington National Cemetery.

President George W. Bush and Civil Unions

President George W. Bush wanted to find a middle ground of compromise by advocating for Civil Unions. Bush backed civil unions but not full marriage equality.

Bush defied his Party and supported Civil Unions in 2004 but that same year, he backed a constitutional amendment forbidding same-sex marriage.

President Bush said, "I don't think we should deny people rights to a civil union, a legal arrangement, if that's what a state chooses to do so."

He was going against the Republican Party official platform that opposed Civil Unions.

However, it remains to be seen if at all President George W Bush would have passed such a law as Texas Governor.

Bush's position was, "I view the definition of marriage different from legal arrangements that enable people to have rights. And I strongly believe that marriage ought to be defined as between a union between a man and a woman. Now, having said that, states ought to be able to have the right to pass laws that enable people to be able to have rights like others."

But his Vice President, Dick Cheney, opposed the constitutional amendment to ban gay marriage, going against popular opinion among social conservatives.

Mr. Cheney, whose daughter Mary is a lesbian, said that he favored the right of states, rather than the federal government, to define marriage. He also said, "freedom means freedom for everyone" to enter "into any kind of relationship they want."

Governor Mitt Romney, the Republican Party presidential candidate in 2012, was even more conservative than George W. Bush. He was against both Civil Unions and same-sex marriages.

LGBTQ Rights Across the World

Across the world, gay rights range from marriage acceptance to punishment by death. As gay rights supporters push for acceptance by society worldwide, the issue is increasingly being framed as a fundamental human right.

The Trump administration has announced a global campaign to end the criminalization of homosexuality in countries where it's still illegal to be gay- mostly concentrated in the Middle East, Africa, and the Caribbean regions.

The International Lesbian, Gay, Bisexual, Trans, and Intersex Association (ILGA) identified 72 nations that still criminalize homosexuality, including eight where it's punishable by death.

U.S. Ambassador to Germany Richard Grenell, the highest-profile openly gay person serving in the Trump administration, will spearhead the effort.

He will work in collaboration with other countries whose laws already allow for gay rights, and global organizations like the United Nations, the European Union and the Organization for Security and Cooperation in Europe.

In late 2011, during remarks in recognition of International Human Rights Day, then-Secretary of State Hillary Clinton said, "Some have suggested that gay rights and human rights are separate and distinct; but, in fact, they are one and the same."

The Netherlands was the first country to recognize same-sex marriage, and twelve other countries mostly in the first world have since recognized same-sex unions.

But in most parts of the world, notably in the Muslim nations and Africa, homosexuality is still considered a criminal offense sentencing those who practice or advocate for LGBTQ rights to prison or capital punishment.

Even in countries where the law is unclear, members LGBTQ community are subjected to enormous societal pressure and in some cases, they are ostracized, bullied and physically threatened with violence.

Russia has also recently seen an increase in attacks against gay people, following nine regions of the country, which have banned the promotion of "homosexual propaganda" among minors.

Uganda's treatment of homosexuals, on the other hand, has been cited as one of the most extreme in a wide range of approaches to gay rights around the world.

The Uganda Anti-Homosexuality Act of 2014 was poised to add harsher punishments for convicted homosexuals, including a death sentence, but was reduced to a life sentence in prison. However, the Constitutional Court of Uganda struck down the Act on procedural grounds.

Homosexuality is already illegal in Uganda and the anti-gay movement is broadly popular among citizens and legislators.

Several world leaders have denounced the harsh stance against gays in Uganda, including South African Archbishop Desmond Tutu who has likened the tough laws homosexuality to apartheid in an open letter to Ugandan lawmakers.

The South African constitution allows same-sex marriage, the first nation on the continent of Africa to do so.

Archbishop Desmond Tutu's Lesbian daughter, Reverend Canon Tutu is married to Professor van Furth, in a same-sex union in the Netherlands.

Reverend Canon Tutu is the Executive Director of the Desmond & Leah Tutu Legacy Foundation and Professor van Furth is a professor in Pediatric Infectious Diseases at the Vrije University in Amsterdam and holds the Desmond Tutu Chair in Medicine at the University.

As a consequence of a perceived harsh treatment of the LGBTQ community across the world, the Obama administration announced at a Geneva summit that the United States would use "all the tools of American diplomacy, including the potent enticement of foreign aid, to promote gay rights around the world."

In a memorandum issued by President Obama in Washington and in a speech by Secretary of State Hillary Rodham Clinton, the administration vowed to actively combat efforts by other nations that criminalize homosexual conduct, abuse gay men, lesbians, bisexuals or transgendered people, or ignore abuse against them.

Then UK Prime Minister David Cameron also suggested that aid could be cut to countries that did not recognize gay rights but was condemned by several African countries where homosexual acts are banned, including Ghana, Uganda, Kenya, Senegal, and Zimbabwe.

Some 41 nations within the 54-member Commonwealth have laws banning homosexual acts.

Many of these laws are a legacy of British colonial rule and up until the year 2003, sodomy was a crime in parts of the United States.

The backlash against Mr. Cameron's remarks was prompt from some of Britain's former African colonies.

Even though homosexual acts are already illegal in Nigeria, the Senate, which is the highest lawmaking chamber in the country moved to strengthen the law against homosexuality in the face of such threats.

Zambia's President Edgar Lungu will not "impose" gay rights on his citizens in exchange for donor aid. He has insisted that Zambians would not accept LGBTQ rights because of the nation's Christian and cultural values. President Lungu says that "Some cultural differences have proved that some of the rights enjoyed in some countries cannot be applied elsewhere such as in Zambia."

Zambia offers very few legal protections to the LGBTQ community. The country's penal code prohibits gay sexual activity and convicted individuals can face imprisonment of up to 14 years.

Nigeria receives about £140m ($220m) a year from the UK, but the President of the Nigerian Senate

said,"If there is any country that does not want to give us aid on account of this, it should keep its aid"

The late President of Ghana, John Atta Mills rejected the UK's threat to cut aid if he refused to legalize homosexuality. Mr. Mills said the UK could not impose its values on Ghana and he would never legalize gay rights.

Ghana received bilateral aid from the UK of about £90m ($144m during the 2010 financial year, of which about £36m was given as general budget support.

The presidential spokesperson of Ghana said of the aid, "If that aid is going to be tied to things that will destroy the moral fiber of society, do you really want that?"

In 2019, Taiwan's parliament passed legislation to legalize same-sex marriage, making it the first country in Asia to do so.

Voters in Taiwan earlier rejected legalizing same-sex marriages in a series of referendums and backed "pro-family" groups' definition of marriage as the union of a man and woman.

Conservative groups asked for the current legislation, which defines marriage as a union between a man and a woman in Taiwan's Civil Code to remain unchanged, while LGBTQ activists asked for the marriage law to be amended to include same-sex couples.

The newly elected president of Brazil Jair Bolsonaro is delivering on his campaign promises to fight "gender ideology" and has erased LGBTQ issues from the agenda of the country's human rights ministry.

Bolsonaro is a former military officer and right-wing politician who in the past made incendiary comments about race and sexual orientation. During the 2011 campaign, Bolsonaro said he was "incapable of loving a homosexual son."

Dozens of gay couples in Brazil rushed to get married in the last month before Bolsonaro took office because they were afraid that the new president would try to limit same-sex marriage.

The newly appointed human rights minister, Damares Alves, is an Evangelical Pastor. He claims that diversity policies have "threatened" family values and has warned that there will be no more ideological indoctrination of children and teenagers in Brazil. Alves said of his new administration that, "Girls will be princesses and boys will be princes".

Hosanna-Tabor Evangelical Lutheran Church and School v. EEOC

In October of 2011, the Obama Justice Department argued before the Supreme Court in the case of Hosanna-Tabor Evangelical Lutheran Church and School v. EEOC (the Equal Employment Opportunity Commission that the ministerial exemption to federal hiring standards should be rescinded.

The school is part of the Lutheran Church-Missouri Synod, the second-largest Lutheran denomination in the United States.

The case involved a teacher in a church-affiliated school who was fired because she threatened to bring an Americans with Disabilities Act (ADA case to protect her rights to continue in her job despite a history of sleep disorders.

Cheryl Perich, who had been a teacher at a school in Redford, Michigan, brought the case forward.

Ms. Perich argued that she was fired for pursuing an employment discrimination claim based on her disability, narcolepsy. Even though she had taught mostly secular subjects, she also taught religion classes and attended chapel services with her class.

Before the Court, was the case whether the Americans with Disabilities Act (ADA protects ministers and other teachers in religious schools or not.

The church's claim was that in her teaching role she was also serving as a minister of the church and that the courts had ruled that the ADA does not apply to ministers.

The revocation of that exemption would mean that churches could be forced to violate their doctrinal beliefs and hire anyone who did not share or uphold such beliefs.

In what became known as a major religious liberty decision, the Supreme Court for the first time recognized a "ministerial exception" to employment discrimination laws, saying that churches and other religious groups must be free to choose their leaders without government interference.

And Supreme Court Chief Justice Roberts devoted part of his opinion to a history of religious freedom in Britain and the United States.

He concluded that an animating principle behind the First Amendment's religious liberty clauses was *"to prohibit government interference in the internal affairs of religious groups generally and in the selection of their leaders in particular".*

He wrote, "The Establishment Clause prevents the government from appointing ministers" and that "the Free Exercise Clause prevents it from interfering with the freedom of religious groups to select their own."

Religious Exemptions on Contraception

Evangelicals and other faith-based groups had another sharp disagreement with the Obama administration on January 20, 2012, angered by a mandate issued by U.S. Department of Health and Human Services requiring organizations to provide contraceptives, sterilization services, and abortion-inducing drugs (such as the morning- after contraceptive pill to its employees).

There was a narrow "religious exemption" clause to this order, but religious charities and hospitals felt that they were required to violate their beliefs and offer these services.

In a demonstration of solidarity, evangelicals and Catholics joined together to protest this example of governmental overreach into religious institutions and to date, there has been no satisfactory resolution of this matter.

In a statement released by the United States Conference of Catholic Bishops, the U.S. Department of Health and Human Services (HHS reaffirmed a rule forcing virtually all-private health care plans to cover sterilization, abortion-inducing drugs, and contraception.

These are listed among "preventive services for women" that all health plans will have to cover without co-pays or other cost sharing, regardless of whether the insurer, the employer or other plan sponsor or even the woman herself objects to such coverage.

 The statement further indicated that the exemption provided for "religious employers" was so narrow that it failed to cover the vast majority of faith-based organizations, including Catholic hospitals, universities, and charities that help millions every year.

The Conference of Catholic Bishops also said that on February 10, 2012, the Obama Administration made this rule final "without change", delayed enforcement for a year against religious nonprofits that were still not exempted (Catholic charities, hospitals, and colleges and promised to develop

more regulations to "accommodate" them by the
end of that additional year.

But that promised "accommodation" still forced
them to pay for "services" that violate their
religious convictions. While the original rule that
violated religious liberty so severely had not been
changed but finalized, the HHS promised some kind
of "accommodation," but only after the 2012
general election.

The Bishops maintained that the promised
"accommodation", even at its best, would still force
their institutions to violate their beliefs and there
would still be no exemption for objecting insurers,
secular employers, for-profit religious employers,
or individuals.

The Bishops rallying point was to mobilize
Catholics and others of good will to fight what they
have characterized as an unprecedented attack on
conscience rights and religious liberty by the
Obama administration for refusing to recognize the
Constitutional conscience rights of organizations
and individuals who oppose the mandate.

The Obama administration included contraception
as part of the minimum coverage requirements for
all healthcare plans under the affordable care Act.

This led to objections from religious based
corporations like the Hobby Lobby and from
nonprofit organizations like the Little Sisters of the

Poor-a Catholic order of nuns that operates nursing homes around the United States, which has a religious affiliation.

The other petitioners include religiously affiliated hospitals, universities, and charities.

Their contention is that the Obama administration's current "accommodation" that has freed them from paying for the contraception coverage but still requires them to inform the government or the insurer for the objection still implicates them, improperly.

Seven of the eight appeals courts that have ruled on the workaround have said it does not impose a "substantial burden" on religious rights and that it does serve a compelling interest in providing health care.

The courts have thus ruled that the workaround does not violate the federal law known as the Religious Freedom Restoration Act.

Before the Supreme Court, lawyer Paul Clement, representing the Little Sisters and other groups, has argued to the contrary, that the workaround is, in fact, a "substantial burden."

"The government itself admits that they can't provide the services unless they get this necessary information from my clients," Clement says. "When you force somebody to pay for somebody else's contraception, including forms of contraception that many religions view as abortifacients ... you are treading on religiously difficult territory."

The petitioners are quoting the same federal law that the federal court used when it made a ruling, in 2014, that for-profit corporations, like the Hobby Lobby, did not need to comply with the regular coverage requirement.

CHAPTER 3

THE CHRISTIAN RIGHT'S INFLUENCE IN AMERICAN POLITICS

Like him or not, the announcement of Donald J Trump entering the US presidential race on Tuesday, June 16, 2015 at Trump Tower in New York City has shaken and changed the status quo of politics not only in the United States, but across the world.

The real estate mogul and reality television star unabashedly criticizes political correctness.
In his speech to announce that he would seek the Republican nomination for President, he said, "We need somebody that literally will take this country and make it great again. We can do that."

At the end of candidate Trump's speech, he said, "Sadly the American dream is dead. But if I get elected president I will bring it back bigger and better and stronger than ever before."
President Trump has postured himself, as the strongman America needs to "make it great again".

At the Republican Convention in the State of Ohio, Mr. Trump's acceptance speech broke with political tradition.

Unlike his Republican predecessors who had made similar speeches, Mr. Trump neither pointed the nation to a collective responsibility to solve America's problems nor did he call on God's help.

For instance, Richard Nixon in 1968 recognized that the nation was torn by war abroad and crime at home. In his acceptance speech, Nixon said, "Without God's help and your help, we will surely fail; but with God's help and your help, we shall surely succeed."

In 1980, Ronald Reagan in accepting his party nomination said, "I ask you not simply to 'Trust me. But to trust your values—our values—and to hold me responsible for living up to them."

In the year 2000, George W. Bush struck a note of humility in his speech. "I know the presidency is an office that turns pride into prayer. But I am eager to start on the work ahead."

Mr. Trump spoke as the embodiment of the nation, and that he would speak and fight for it as its sole hope for redemption. He unequivocally declared, "I am your voice. I alone can fix it. I will restore law and order."

The backdrop to Mr. Trump's promises was that America as a nation is in crisis and suffers from domestic disaster beset by "poverty and violence at home" full of shuttered factories and crushed communities.

Internationally, America has suffered a lot of humiliation of "war and destruction abroad" and that attacks on law enforcement officers at home and terrorism threaten the American way of life.

Mr. Trump's message of America first, and for Americans, struck a nerve. It renewed a new sense of hope in communities that have been economically devastated by the loss of jobs through outsourcing- a practice in which companies close shop in the US to manufacture the same products cheaper elsewhere and bring them back for sale on America's domestic markets.

He promised an economic-development measure that would punish companies that globally outsource jobs and move operations offshore.

He equally promised incentives and rewards for firms that maintain jobs in the United States.

"It's both a carrot and a stick," President Trump said. "It is an incentive to stay. But it is perhaps even more so—if you leave, it's going to be very tough for you to think that you're going to be able to sell your product back into our country."

Trump also touched on the deplorable conditions in America's inner cities by promising job growth, law and order, and school choice.

During a campaign trail in Michigan in August of 2016, candidate Trump promised prosperity and safety back to America's inner city communities.

"Look at how much African American communities are suffering from Democratic control. To those, I say the following: What do you have to lose by trying something new like Trump? What do you have to lose?" he asked. "You live in your poverty, your schools are no good, you have no jobs, 58 percent of your youth is unemployed. What the hell do you have to lose?"

As in many major American cities, violent crime is a problem. Citing the number of Chicago shootings and murders as the highest in 2016 and 2017, President Trump threatened to intervene in Chicago's law enforcement by sending in the Feds to stop the carnage.

The Political Influence of the Christian Right

One of the unlikely stalwart supporters of President Trump is the Evangelical Christian right, also referred to the Religious Right.

A two-year collaboration between the National Association of Evangelicals (NAE and Nashville-based LifeWay Research was conducted to improve how researchers quantify Evangelicals in surveys.

The final report defines Evangelicals by theology as people of faith defined by the beliefs rather than by self-identity, denominational affiliation, race or politics.

For example, the African American Protestant population is overwhelmingly Evangelical in theology and orientation, but is often left out and separated from polls seeking to identify the political preferences of Evangelicals.

Based on this protocol of research, 53% of Evangelicals said they voted for Donald Trump in 2016 compared to 46% for Mitt Romney in 2012, 49% for John McCain in 2008, 68 and 69% for George W. Bush in 2000 and 2004 respectively, and 45% Bob Dole in 1996.

The survey found that "only half of Evangelical voters characterized their vote as voting for their specific candidate" in 2016, leading researchers to conclude that US Evangelicals are "more issue-oriented than candidate-focused."

 In 2016, many evangelicals looked past a candidate as an individual to vote for a specific issue, platform, or party a candidate represented, seeing the candidates more like objects of representation than as individuals whose values and ideals fit theirs.

The position that many Evangelical Christians who support President Trump is reflected in the words spoken by Jerry Falwell Jr., "We are not electing a pastor-in-chief, we are choosing a president." Jerry Falwell Jr. is the President of Liberty University, a Christian University, and a devout supporter of Mr. Trump's candidacy.

He described Mr. Trump as a blue-collar billionaire because of his love for ordinary Americans, generosity, and boldness.

In his endorsement, Jerry Falwell Jr. likened candidate Trump's qualities to those of Winston Churchill.

Just like Winston Churchill, Mr. Trump would put his country first and never surrender to a world that has become increasingly hostile to evangelical values.

Electing the Trump and Indiana Governor Mike Pence ticket would ensure that the next few appointments of justices on the Supreme Court were conservative, strict-constructionist, pro-life, and would uphold the Second Amendment right to bear arms.

The presence of Governor Pence as Vice President on the Trump campaign was a bonus for the religious right.

Evangelicals across the country, based on his record on abortion and religious freedom, have likened

Pence to a prophet restoring conservative Christianity to its rightful place and an evangelical-Christian worldview at the center of public policy and American life.

Falwell Jr. also believed that the vote for Trump was a vote for "more freedom and less government, a vote for national security and responsible immigration policy, a vote to finally fight radical Islamic Terrorism and to rebuild America's respect abroad".

Mr. Trump's candidacy was sold as a non-establishment Republican and strong leader, unafraid to call out and confront America's enemies, while President Obama and candidate Hillary Clinton's leadership was deemed weak and their policies failed to defeat Terrorism, notwithstanding their unwillingness to call radical Islamic Terrorism by name.

Mr. Trump enjoys support from some of the leading white Evangelical leaders of tremendous influence in Church circles, not only in the United States but across the world also.

Some Evangelicals have likened Mr. Trump's rise to power and his role to that of King of Persia, Cyrus the Great, whom Isaiah prophesied in chapter forty-five in the Bible.

Although Cyrus the Great was a heathen, God would use him as a royal savior or "messiah" to be the agent to bring about the restoration of Jerusalem and would destroy Babylon, the oppressor of the Jews.

Similarly, although Mr. Trump lacked in some traditional evangelical qualities of moral leadership and integrity, many Evangelical believers embraced him, as their "Cyrus" in bringing back the religious freedoms that were apparently lost under the Obama administration.

Falwell Jr. argues that this position is not hypocritical for Evangelical leaders to support a leader who has advocated violence and who has committed adultery and lies often.

 He believes that "When Jesus said we're all sinners, he really meant all of us, everybody. I don't think you can choose a president based on their personal behavior… you choose a president based on what their policies are. That's why I don't think it's hypocritical."

Other Evangelical leaders, however, have remained critical of Jerry Falwell Jr. continued support for the president, saying he needs to demand higher moral and ethical standards of the president.

Falwell disagrees and says, "It may be immoral for them not to support him because he's got African American employment to record highs, Hispanic employment to record highs. They need to look at what the president did for the poor. A lot of the people who criticized me, because they had a hard time stomaching supporting someone who owned casinos and strip clubs or whatever, a lot of them have come around and said, 'Yeah, you were right."

CHAPTER 4

IDENTITY POLITICS AND THE DEEPENING EVANGELICAL DIVISION

From the surface of it, the two make strange bedfellows. Mr. Trump's personal and moral demeanor on many social and religious issues is opposite to what Evangelicals believe.

However, in President Trump, many Evangelicals have found an ally in rolling back some of the "religious freedoms" they felt were eroded in American politics. On May 3rd, 2018, President Trump signed an Executive Order meant "to ensure that the faith-based and community organizations that form the bedrock of our society have strong advocates in the White House and throughout the Federal Government."

The Order was also meant to affirm that, "President Trump has publicly stood with people of faith and with those who advocate for the sanctity of life and that throughout his tenure as President, Donald Trump has been a champion for religious liberty in the United States, restoring the ideals that have under-girded our Nation's freedom and prosperity since its founding."

President Trump has become a strong ally of a section of Evangelical Christians in rolling back abortion rights and a possible repeal of Rowe v. Wade (a 1973 landmark US Supreme Court decision on the issue of the laws that criminalized or restricted access to abortion).

President Trump is also scaling back Lesbian, Gay, Bi-Sexual, Transgender, and Queer (LGBTQ) rights.

For example, President Donald J. Trump issued an ultimatum to the Pentagon to stop enlisting Transgender Americans to serve in the Army.

Immigration and its handling is perhaps one of the main issues that has deepened the political divide among Evangelical Christians in the United States.

At the center of the controversy, is the so-called caravan of asylum seekers who are believed to be fleeing Central America because of poverty and violence.

Opponents of the harsh treatment of immigrants at the Southern border insist that there is more to the policy of keeping America safe than meets the eye.

They have suggested that it also has everything to do with the fact that, demographically, the United States is no longer a majority white Christian country.

73

At 45 percent of the population, white Christians are now a shrinking demographic and this new reality has tremendous social and political consequences, which affects the future direction of the United States.

Electing Mr. Trump and his America first campaign was also about restoring a sense of belonging and understanding of a country they have become used to.

A sense of country is lost when you are no longer the majority demographic in the politics of the nation.

White Evangelical Protestants are a unique exception in their overwhelming support for the president. Almost seven in ten (68%) of white Evangelical Protestants have a favorable view of President Trump, and 28% have a very favorable view, including immigration.

By contrast, the majorities of all other major religious groups have an unfavorable opinion of President Trump. For example, Majorities of black Protestants (80%), religiously unaffiliated Americans (75%), Hispanic Catholics (74%), non-Christian-religious Americans (73%), white mainline Protestants (52%), and white Catholics (52%) have a negative opinion of President Trump's views.

Ed Stetzer is the Executive Director of the Billy Graham Center at Wheaton College. He believes that, repeatedly, the Bible instructs us to welcome and protect foreigners and that President Trump has fueled fears about immigration to take advantage of Evangelicals.

He writes, "Regardless of political affiliation and positions, Evangelicals need to see this culture of fear of others for what it is: un-Christian"

But Tony Perkins, president of the Conservative Family Research Council and an ally of President Trump has a praised President Trump's hardline stance on immigration.

He believes, in contrast, that the divine directive for Christians to care for the poor and immigrant has limits.

Perkins view is that, "Scripture does speak to the poor, it does speak to the immigrant, but it also speaks to the rule of law. In fact, in almost every instance you read in the Old Testament about taking in the poor, immigrant and stranger, it is then that they have an obligation to operate by your customs and laws. It's the assimilation, it's the rule of law."

On foreign policy, one third or 15 million, of all Evangelicals in the United States have a prophetic interest in the future of the nation of Israel.

75

They believe in the end times and a future Second coming and a physical rule of Christ on earth. They also believe that Christ's return will be preceded by natural disasters and wars, the rise of the antichrist, and the great tribulation.

At the end of that period of anguish, Christ will appear, evil will be defeated, and Israel will be restored.

At the end of this period, Jews will convert to Christ and the great millennium rule will begin, and the restoration of Jerusalem, as a historic and biblical capital, is critical and central to God's promise for a Holy land for Jews on both sides of the Jordan River.

The Trump administration recognized Jerusalem as the capital of Israel, a move supported by 53% of American Evangelicals and only 40% opposed it. Overall, 63% of all Americans opposed the decision.

Although Jews have their own theology of the end time, and quite different from the Evangelical version, they nevertheless still welcome the political support from the United States and from Evangelicals in particular.

Another moment of great division within the Evangelical leadership ranks was the aftermath of the "Unite the Right" rally in Charlottesville where several leading names in the white-nationalist alt-right movement were featured in an open display of identity politics.

These marches also attracted white-nationalists displaying Nazi symbols and chanting "blood and soil" (the English translation of the Nazi slogan).

The incident in which James A. Fields, a member of the fascist group American Vanguard, deliberately rammed a car into a crowd of counter-protesters killing 32-year-old Heather Heyer created a nationwide outrage.

During a news conference, while he condemned white supremacists, President Trump defended some "fine people" in Charlottesville and asked why the "alt-left" had not been criticized for violence.

In a first for his Evangelical advisory council, New York City mega church pastor A.R. Bernard announced he was stepping down from the unofficial board of Evangelical advisers to President Trump.

Pastor Bernard cited a "deepening conflict in values" between himself and the administration and called the Evangelical Advisory Board board a "photo op" and urged white Evangelical leaders to hold the president "accountable to an agenda."

"I think that as time progressed you, look for change, you look for consistency, you look for responsibility and leadership and I didn't see consistency in a set of core values that influenced and shaped his thinking. And when he vacillated over the last week, especially over Charlottesville, I had come to the point where I had to make a decision to more than just step away. I had to fully disengage myself. When you vacillate like that, it means that there's not a set of core values that you have determined to guide your thinking, your decision-making. Instead, it demonstrates that you are being tossed between opinions of those around you. And I've got a problem with that kind of lack of leadership." Pastor Bernard said.

Other leaders remained on the Advisory Council, including Southern Baptist pastor Robert Jeffress who tweeted, "Honored to serve @POTUS on his Faith Initiative Council. He has done more in 6 mo. to protect religious liberty than any pres. in history"

Another Sothern Baptist Pastor, Jack Graham, tweeted "The self-righteous condemned Jesus for loving sinners and hanging out with them. We should never fail to love the people He loves".

Tony Suarez of the National Hispanic Christian Leadership Conference "Could you imagine Daniel, Jeremiah, Samuel, Nathan, or Isaiah saying they'd no longer advise or speak to the king or government?"

Televangelist Pastor Mark Burns also tweeted, "Calls for Me to RESIGN...If God called me to support and Advise @realDonaldTrump spiritually How Can you Resign?"

Jonathan Falwell, who leads the mega church Thomas Road Baptist Church in Lynchburg, VA. and Jerry Falwell Jr., who leads Liberty University, are blood brothers.

The deepening divide on identity politics among Evangelicals was further demonstrated in how the two brothers responded very differently from one another concerning the events in Charlottesville.

Pastor Jonathan denounced racism from his pulpit during a Sunday service, but his brother remained silent for several days and later tweeted "Finally a leader in WH. Jobs returning, N Korea backing down, bold truthful stmt about #charlottesville tragedy. So proud of @realdonaldtrump"

The Rise of the Christian Left

Another growing phenomenon in American politics is the Christian left also known as the Religious Left and it has increased its activism since the election of President Trump.

Although not as powerful and prominent as the Religious Right, it has recently gained more prominence by coming out more in the public square of national politics.

The Religious left mainly consists of progressive Protestant and Catholic believers- mainly organizing on social issues such as immigration reform, healthcare, and welfare.

For example, the number of churches volunteering to offer help and sanctuary has rapidly increased.

The Religious Left is not new; it has always been part of American history.

It has in the past played key roles in marching and praying for the abolition of institutional slavery, and the promotion of civil rights and labor reforms.

In recent history, it has extended its platform to include gun violence prevention and LGBTQ rights.

The Religious Left has also forged meaningful alliances with American Muslim and Jewish groups on specific issues such as immigration or hate-incidents.

For instance, interfaith leaders, including the Quakers, Rabbis, and Imams, have recently demonstrated at the San Diego-Tijuana border.

They have protested the militarization of the US-Mexico border by putting their bodies on the line in support of migrants' right to seek asylum.

The premise of these demonstrations by the Faith leaders is that " A nation must protect its borders, but more importantly, a nation must protect its soul."

Similar resistance was applied against Reverend Franklin Graham by Vancouver Mayor Gregor Robertson and 14 local leaders from Evangelical, Anglican, Roman Catholic and other Christian groups.

The Vancouver leaders came together to discourage Reverend Graham from coming to preach at the Festival of Hope in Vancouver Canada, which was scheduled in March of 2017.

They accused Reverend Graham of being a polarizing figure who has made denigrating remarks to Muslims and the LGBTQ.

Reverend Graham was criticized as being "insensitive" for supporting a law Russian President Vladimir Putin signed in 2013 to protect minors (children) in Russia from homosexuals promoting their lifestyle, and more specifically, the law bans the "propaganda of nontraditional sexual relations to minors."

Minority groups have questioned Reverend Graham's unwavering support for President Trump, of whom Graham said, " He did everything wrong, politically. He offended gays. He offended women. He offended the military. He offended black people. He offended the Hispanic people. He offended everybody! And he became president of the United States. Only God could do that."

The Vancouver Christian leaders' view was that "Given that the express goal of this event is evangelism, with the commitment of new believers to Christ, we do not believe that Rev. Graham, with his expressed broader belief system, should be the exemplar that impresses itself upon these new believers."

In July of 2015, four innocent United States Marines were killed in Chattanooga, Tennessee. The killer was 24-year-old Mohammad Yousuf Abdulazeez, born in Kuwait, had Jordanian citizenship and was a naturalized United States citizen. He was carrying an AK-47 type of weapon with 30-round magazines when he opened fire.

Reverend Graham reacted to this sad news by posting the following message on his Facebook page:

"We are under attack by Muslims at home and abroad. We should stop all immigration of Muslims to the U.S. until this threat with Islam has been settled. Every Muslim that comes into this country has the potential to be radicalized – and they do their killing to honor their religion and Muhammad. During World War 2, we didn't allow the Japanese to immigrate to America, nor did we allow Germans. Why are we allowing Muslims now? Do you agree? Let your Congressman know that we've got to put a stop to this and close the floodgates."

Reverend Graham was also in support of President Trump's 90 days ban for people from 7 predominantly Muslim nations from entering the United States.

Reverend Franklin Graham has reached many people for Christ over the years through evangelism, following the footsteps of his late father, the world-renowned evangelist Billy Graham.

He also runs a charity organization called the Samaritan's Purse, which brings aid and medical relief to people all over the world, including in many Muslim-majority nations.

The Samaritan's Purse has operated in the Middle East for over 30 years, providing assistance such as food, heaters, blankets, coats, shelter plastic, and more for tens of thousands of refugees.

The organization has also opened a 54-bed field trauma hospital in northern Iraq where the wounded are treated in the fight over Mosul.

CHAPTER 5

THE BIBLICAL STRUCTURES OF GOVERNMENT

Only God has the unlimited authority of Government.

[16] For by Him all things were created that are in heaven and that are on earth, visible and invisible, whether thrones or dominions or principalities or powers. All things were created through Him and for Him. [17] And He is before all things, and in Him all things consist. Col 1: 16-17

[3] who being the brightness of *His* glory and the express image of His person, and upholding all things by the word of His power, when He had by Himself purged our sins, sat down at the right hand of the Majesty on high. Hebrews 1:3

God's system of government is delegated to: self (individual), family, Church and State or Civil governments.

Government, therefore, cannot be defined exclusively in political terms.

Isaiah 9:6-7 states:

[6] For unto us a Child is born,
Unto us a Son is given;
And the government will be upon His shoulder.
And His name will be called
Wonderful, Counselor, Mighty God,
Everlasting Father, Prince of Peace.
[7] Of the increase of *His* government and peace
There will be no end,
Upon the throne of David and over His kingdom,
To order it and establish it with judgment and justice
From that time forward, even forever.
The zeal of the LORD of hosts will perform this.

Christ is the Head of the Church, which is His Body on earth. "And the government will be upon His shoulder" implies that the establishment and instruction of God's principles in self, family, Church and civil governments rest upon the Church.

Self-Government

All human government begins at the individual level.

Self-government or self-control is the bedrock and undergirds all institutional governments of the family, Church, and the State.

Without self-government or control, all the other institutional governments of family, Church, and

State will be comprised, reflecting the corruption of the individual.

Self-government deals with individual behavior and character. In the absence of self -control the following character flaws are evident:

[19] Now the works of the flesh are evident, which are: adultery, fornication, uncleanness, lewdness,

[20] idolatry, sorcery, hatred, contentions, jealousies, outbursts of wrath, selfish ambitions, dissensions, heresies,

[21] envy, murders, drunkenness, revelries, and the like; of which I tell you beforehand, just as I also told *you* in time past, that those who practice such things will not inherit the kingdom of God. Galatians 5:19-21

On the other hand, self-government can be judged by the following character traits:

[22] But the fruit of the Spirit is love, joy, peace, longsuffering, kindness, goodness, faithfulness, [23] gentleness, self-control. Against such there is no law. Galatians 5:22-23

In 1682, William Penn wrote, "Let men be good and government cannot be bad, if it is ill they will cure it. But if men be bad, let the government be never so good, they will endeavor to warp and spoil it to their turn."

Family Government

It takes self-controlled people to make marriage work according to God's intended plan for the family.

Husbands are expected to love their wives as Christ Himself loves His Church.

 Wives also are instructed in their conduct that would result in a successful marriage unit, based on the principle of giving in to each other.

[22] Wives, submit to your own husbands, as to the Lord.

[23] For the husband is head of the wife, as also Christ is head of the church; and He is the Savior of the body.

[24] Therefore, just as the church is subject to Christ, so *let* the wives *be* to their own husbands in everything.

[25] Husbands, love your wives, just as Christ also loved the church and gave Himself for her. Ephesians 5: 22-25

Parents in the family unit have a moral authority to discipline their children and raise them in the teachings of the faith.

Children, obey your parents in the Lord, for this is right.

 [2] "Honor your father and mother," which is the first commandment with promise: [3] "that it may be well with you and you may live long on the earth." [4] And you,

fathers, do not provoke your children to wrath, but bring them up in the training and admonition of the Lord. Ephesians 6:1-4

Church Government

God has instituted Church leaders, elders and deacons to hold authority in the local assembly.

They are men and women whose characters are proven and their homes are properly managed.

Leaders in the Church should fulfill the Biblical requirements of character in order to exercise the authority to teach, conduct sacraments and discipline members.

The basis for continued ministry is consistent commitment to character.

Church leaders are to be spiritually prepared, socially gracious, living in domestic order and personal holiness.

Being a leader in a secular setting does not automatically translate into Church leadership.

This *is* a faithful saying: If a man desires the position of a bishop, he desires a good work.

[2] A bishop then must be blameless, the husband of one wife, temperate, sober-minded, of good behavior, hospitable, able to teach; [3] not given to wine, not violent,

not greedy for money, but gentle, not quarrelsome, not covetous; [4] one who rules his own house well, having *his* children in submission with all reverence [5] (for if a man does not know how to rule his own house, how will he take care of the church of God?); [6] not a novice, lest being puffed up with pride he fall into the *same* condemnation as the devil. [7] Moreover he must have a good testimony among those who are outside, lest he fall into reproach and the snare of the devil. 1Timothy3:1-7

State Government

This is the realm of government that many Christians generally know very little or nothing about.

In some extreme teachings, Christians have been taught to have nothing to do with participating in this realm of government.

This is because partisan politics, considered as "dirty", are exercised in this realm of State or Civil government.

It is God himself, who has created this form of government just as He did the individual, family, and the Church.

Let every soul be subject to the governing authorities. For there is no authority except from God, and God appoints the authorities that exist.

[2] Therefore whoever resists the authority resists the ordinance of God, and those who resist will bring judgment on themselves.

[3] For rulers are not a terror to good works, but to evil. Do you want to be unafraid of the authority? Do what is good, and you will have praise from the same.

[4] For he is God's minister to you for good. But if you do evil, be afraid; for he does not bear the sword in vain; for he is God's minister, an avenger to *execute* wrath on him who practices evil.

[5] Therefore *you* must be subject, not only because of wrath but also for conscience' sake.

[6] For because of this you also pay taxes, for they are God's ministers attending continually to this very thing. [7] Render therefore to all their due: taxes to whom taxes *are due,* customs to whom customs, fear to whom fear, honor to whom honor. Romans 13: 1-7

And,

[13] Therefore submit yourselves to every ordinance of man for the Lord's sake, whether to the king as supreme, [14] or to governors, as to those who are sent by him for the punishment of evildoers and *for the* praise of those who do good. 1Peter 2: 13-14

From the above scriptures we can deduce the following:

1. All authority is established by God. Man can, however, create illegitimate or perverted authority.

2. Civil rulers exercise political authority by God's decree (they are God's ministers). This does not necessary mean that God places every ruler in office there.

God ordains the civil office and authority but the individual holding the office may not necessarily be God's choice!

Christians will be subject to civil authorities only as far as their fundamental rights to freedom of worship and association and the exercise of a free conscience based on their Biblical beliefs are not denied.

When Moses was overwhelmed with the task of leading the Israelites into the desert on their way to the land of promise Canaan, his father in law Jethro stepped in and advised him to choose men of high caliber with whom to govern the people.

[21] Moreover you shall select from all the people able men, such as fear God, men of truth, hating covetousness; and place *such* over them *to be* rulers of thousands, rulers of hundreds, rulers of fifties, and rulers of tens. Exodus 18:21

When upright men and women run the civil government, nations prosper and people live in peace.

[34] Righteousness exalts a nation, But sin *is* a reproach to *any* people Proverbs 14:34

[2] When the righteous are in authority, the people rejoice; But when a wicked *man* rules, the people groan. Proverbs 29:2

[12] Blessed *is* the nation whose God *is* the LORD, The people He has chosen as His own inheritance. Psalms 33:12

[14] Righteousness and justice *are* the foundation of Your throne; Mercy and truth go before Your face. Psalms 89:14

CHAPTER 6

BIBLICAL ROLES OF THE STATE GOVERNMENT

The State government has a role to play, different but complementary to that of the family and the Church.

The State has no authority to perform the tasks meant for the Church and the family and individual liberties given by God.

Neither is the Church called to supplant the authority and responsibility of the State and the family.

Here are some major responsibilities of the State in the Bible:

Collection of Tax

State Governments have a Biblical responsibility to collect taxes from all its citizens who are eligible to pay. The money collected is primarily meant to establish a good infrastructure system and services to enhance productivity among citizens.

[16] And they sent to Him their disciples with the Herodians, saying, "Teacher, we know that You are true, and teach the way of God in truth; nor do You care about anyone, for You do not regard the person of men. [17] Tell us, therefore, what do You think? Is it lawful to pay taxes to Caesar, or not?" [18] But Jesus perceived their wickedness, and said, "Why do you test Me, *you* hypocrites? [19] Show Me the tax money." So they brought Him a denarius. [20] And He said to them, "Whose image and inscription *is* this?"[21] They said to Him, "Caesar's." And He said to them, "Render therefore to Caesar the things that are Caesar's, and to God the things that are God's. Matthew 22:21

And

[7] Render therefore to all their due: taxes to whom taxes *are due,* customs to whom customs, fear to whom fear, honor to whom honor. Romans 13:7

The role of State government is to create an enabling environment and give incentives for its citizens to improve their lives and nation through innovation and hard work.

People should not only be taught how to catch fish, but they must have access to the fishpond as well.

Taxes imposed on people should be reasonable and not overbearing.

While many State governments around the world have social safety nets and welfare programs for the disadvantaged and disabled, the primary responsibility to provide and feed the family lays at the family level.

[8] But if anyone does not provide for his own, and especially for those of his household, he has denied the faith and is worse than an unbeliever. 1Tomothy 5: 8

Jesus Himself said the poor would always be with us. (Matthew 26:11)

The Church has a primary mandate in helping cushion and alleviates poverty by giving a hand up, not a handout, through social safety nets in conjunction with Not-for-profit organizations.

The gospel call is about doing good deeds to the "least among us".

[34] Then the King will say to those on His right hand, 'Come, you blessed of My Father, inherit the kingdom prepared for you from the foundation of the world:

[35] for I was hungry and you gave Me food; I was thirsty and you gave Me drink; I was a stranger and you took Me in; [36] I *was* naked and you clothed Me; I was sick and you visited Me; I was in prison and you came to Me.'[37] "Then the righteous will answer Him, saying, 'Lord, when did we see You hungry and feed *You,* or thirsty and give *You* drink? [38] When did we see You a stranger and take *You* in, or naked and clothe *You?* [39] Or when did we see You sick, or in prison, and come to You?'

[40] And the King will answer and say to them, 'Assuredly, I say to you, inasmuch as you did *it* to one of the least of these My brethren, you did *it* to Me. Matthew 25:34-40

The Church has a duty to teach people how to be productive.

Christians should not be preoccupied with getting to heaven only but must be taught how to be successful here on earth.

God's mandate for man is to have dominion over all of God's creation.

No one is insignificant; we all carry God's identity, imprint, ability, and purpose.

God has given every human with a unique gifting according to His measure.
Individuals should freely innovate and operate for profit in a competitive system with minimum and common sense regulation by Civil government.

A strong business and entrepreneurial sector is the economic engine of a nation.

The Bible teaches the principles of free enterprise. For example, in the parable of the talents, it can be seen that the master was pleased with his servants who used the talents he gave them to gain more. (Luke 19: 12-27)

God intends for His people to prosper in all things.

[2] Beloved, I pray that you may prosper in all things and be in health, just as your soul prospers. 3 John 2

When the people of Israel entered Canaan the land of promise, Joshua their leader divided the land among the tribes and their families as an inheritance.

Each allocation became private property.

Through policing and community participation, the safety of private property is secure and respected.

In the Ten Commandments, man is required not to steal or covet another man's property.

[15] You shall not steal. [16] "You shall not bear false witness against your neighbor. [17] "You shall not covet your neighbor's house; you shall not covet your neighbor's wife, nor his male servant, nor his female servant, nor his ox, nor his donkey, nor anything that *is* your neighbor's. Exodus 20: 15, 17

Provision of Weights and measures

In the conduct of commerce, the State should ensure that the rules are fair and apply to everyone so that all citizens get a fair reward for their goods and services.

This is pleasing to the Lord. The government should ensure that its citizens own genuine and honest scales and measures when they conduct their

97

business and prevent cheating, false advertising, and pilfering.

[11]Dishonest scales *are* an abomination to the LORD, But a just weight *is* His delight. Proverbs 11:1

[36] You shall have honest scales, honest weights, an honest ephah, and an honest hin: I *am* the LORD your God, who brought you out of the land of Egypt. Leviticus 19:36

[13] You shall not have in your bag differing weights, a heavy and a light. [14] You shall not have in your house differing measures, a large and a small. [15] You shall have a perfect and just weight, a perfect and just measure, that your days may be lengthened in the land which the LORD your God is giving you. Deuteronomy 25: 13-15

Establishing the Judicial System

An independent judicial system should be established based on the appeals court system.

The local and magistrate courts handle lesser matters than the high and supreme courts.

The basis of law and its source in any given society reflects on the "God" of that society.

The law and its interpretation must be fair and should not be used to kill justice, in some cases, for financial gain.

[22] And let them judge the people at all times. Then it will be *that* every great matter they shall bring to you, but every small matter they themselves shall judge. So it will be easier for you, for they will bear *the burden* with you. Exodus 18:22

Anyone who feels that justice has been denied can appeal for redress in a higher court.

God entrusts great responsibility to those who administer justice to do it fairly without delay.

Justice delayed can be justice denied.

God is the final and ultimate judge of all humanity:

[22] (For the LORD *is* our Judge,
The LORD *is* our Lawgiver,
The LORD *is* our King;
He will save us) Isaiah 33:22

National Defense

The State is obligated to defend its citizens against national and international enemies. (Romans13:14).

 Peace is desirable and ought to be our first line of defense.

[18] If it is possible, as much as depends on you, live peaceably with all men. Romans 12:18

However, the world has some ill-intended people whose only objective is to do harm by stealing through occupation, disrupting our freedoms and way of life.

Each nation, therefore, must prepare itself for the possibility of armed conflict.

It is for this reason that the Biblical symbol of authority of the State is the sword (Romans 13:4) and that of the family is the rod (Proverbs 29:15) and that of Church leaders is the power of binding and loosing through prayer. (Matthew16: 19, 18:15-20).

Peace cannot just be defined in terms of the absence of war.

As Christians, we are to pray for peace with a clear understanding that God is the source of our protection.

[2] Therefore I exhort first of all that supplications, prayers, intercessions, *and* giving of thanks be made for all men, [2] for kings and all who are in authority, that we may lead a quiet and peaceable life in all godliness and reverence. 1Timothy 2: 1-2

Freedom of Worship and assembly

Many erroneously believe that the State should be neutral (or secular) on matters of religion and morality. Nothing can be as farther from the truth as such a belief.

The Apostle Paul expected the Roman government to protect him from those who threatened his life because he preached the gospel of our Lord Jesus Christ.

[10] So Paul said, "I stand at Caesar's judgment seat, where I ought to be judged. To the Jews I have done no wrong, as you very well know. [11] For if I am an offender, or have committed anything deserving of death, I do not object to dying; but if there is nothing in these things of which these men accuse me, no one can deliver me to them. I appeal to Caesar. Acts 25: 10-11

Apostle Paul asks us to pray for all men, leaders and those in authority so that we can live in peace and quiet, guaranteeing our freedom to preach the gospel.

This environment "*is* good and acceptable in the sight of God our Savior, who desires all men to be saved and to come to the knowledge of the truth."

Therefore I exhort first of all that supplications, prayers, intercessions, and giving of thanks be made for all men, 2 for kings and all who are in authority, that we may lead a quiet and peaceable life in all godliness and reverence. 3 For this is good and acceptable in the sight of God our Savior, 4 who desires all men to be saved and to come to the knowledge of the truth. 5 For there is one God and one Mediator between God and men, the Man Christ Jesus,

101

6 who gave Himself a ransom for all, to be testified in due time, [7] for which I was appointed a preacher and an apostle—I am speaking the truth in Christ *and* not lying—a teacher of the Gentiles in faith and truth. [8] I desire therefore that the men pray everywhere, lifting up holy hands, without wrath and doubting. 1 Timothy 2:1-8

CHAPTER 7

POLITICS ABHORS A VACUUM

Nature abhors a vacuum. Nature fills every empty space with something, even if that something is colorless and odorless air.

Similarly, politics has no vacuum. It is always possessed and filled by an ideology or worldview.

The battleground is in the mindset of the general populace and who controls it.

Therefore, Christians cannot react to politics just through protest but by proactive engagement.

Consequently, the Apostle Paul writes that as Christians we ought to be filled with all the fullness of God, lest we allow for a vacuum and be filled with something else other than God.

[14] For this reason I bow my knees to the Father of our Lord Jesus Christ, [15] from whom the whole family in heaven and earth is named, [16] that He would grant you, according to the riches of His glory, to be strengthened with might through His Spirit in the inner man, [17] that Christ may dwell in your hearts through faith; that you,

being rooted and grounded in love, [18] may be able to comprehend with all the saints what *is* the width and length and depth and height— [19] to know the love of Christ which passes knowledge; that you may be filled with all the fullness of God. Ephesians 3:14-19

Individually, we are to become relevant and significant.

We are challenged to accept the responsibility of being citizens by getting involved, giving time and effort into the rebuilding of our nations based on God's blueprint.

Democracy

Is there such a reality as the separation of Religion or faith from politics or the affairs of the State?

While Democracy offers the best framework for governance known to man, is it not the elected officials that bring their belief system or faith, or a lack thereof, by which to govern?

Is there such a condition as a secular State or is that not, in and of itself, a belief system? Can there be neutrality of faith in public policy?

Democracy has been touted as the most practical system of government and as the standard measure of good governance in open and progressive societies.

Democracy originates from two Greek words, namely; "Demos" which means "people" and "Kratos" for "rule of the people".

Democracy is a "game" of numbers and the laws are based on the will of the majority.

Democracy is also based on the presumption that the majority is always right. But the nature of humanity is at times inclined to abandon self-restraint for self-satisfaction.

Therefore, Democracy can be a "double-edged" sword. When the whims and fancies of the majority change, the laws change as well.

This is the confluence where Democracy and Faith often clashes. Democracy works by compromise. While the majority may vote to legalize divisive issues such as abortion or same-sex marriage, the faith-based communities, informed by their religious beliefs will oppose such laws. The backlash is reversed when people of faith exert their values.

On November 19, 1863 President Abraham Lincoln went to the battlefield at Gettysburg, Pennsylvania.

He went there to dedicate it as a Soldiers' National Cemetery four and a half months after the Union armies defeated those of the confederacy at the battle of Gettysburg.

The Battle of Gettysburg occurred over summer days, between July 1 and July 3, 1863 around the small market town of Gettysburg, Pennsylvania.

What may have begun as a skirmish ended up involving 160,000 Americans and effectively decided the fate of the Union.

In just over two minutes he delivered a speech, which became known as one of the best in American history.

Within this short time, President Lincoln reiterated the principles of human equality enshrined in the Declaration of Independence and described the Civil war as a struggle for the preservation of the Union.

Over time, this speech with its ending – government of the People, by the People, for the People - has come to symbolize the definition of democracy itself:

"…. that this nation, under God, shall have a new birth of freedom -- and that government of the people, by the people, for the people, shall not perish from the earth."

In immature and wannabe democracies, however, there is the tendency to make "the government of the people, by the people, for the people" become "the government over the people, in the name of the people".

In established democracies, minority groups and interests can be given special protective status because their genuine causes cannot see the light of day in the game of numbers.

The exercise of democracy requires great maturity to handle unity in diversity. Unity should not swallow up diversity and neither should diversity be at the expense of unity. Democracy only works by a give-and-take compromise of divergent views. Also, democratic leaders must only promise what they can do and do what they promise.

Within a constitutional democracy and process, Christians have the right to demand and declare that the laws that govern their nations reflect the fundamental principles of God's word.

These include the upholding the exercise of individual freedoms and liberty, good family values, and free enterprise based on the Biblical values that all human life, including unborn babies, is sacred before God our creator.

[3] Behold, children *are* a heritage from the LORD, the fruit of the womb *is* a reward. [4] Like arrows in the hand of a warrior, so *are* the children of one's youth. Psalm 127: 3-4

[13] For You formed my inward parts; you covered me in my mother's womb. [14] I will praise You, for I am fearfully *and* wonderfully made; Marvelous are Your works, And *that* my soul knows very well.

[15] My frame was not hidden from You, When I was made in secret, *And* skillfully wrought in the lowest parts of the earth. [16] Your eyes saw my substance, being yet unformed. And in Your book they all were written, The days fashioned for me, When *as yet there were* none of them. [17] How precious also are Your thoughts to me, O God! How great is the sum of them! [18] *If* I should count them, they would be more in number than the sand; When I awake, I am still with You.
Psalm 139: 13-18

The family is the most basic unit in the building block of a strong society and that marriage between one woman and man is upheld as a divine and sacred order.

When God's order in the home is destroyed, the nation cannot potentially stand strong.

[4] And He answered and said to them, "Have you not read that He who made *them* at the beginning 'made them male and female,' [5] and said, 'For this reason a man shall leave his father and mother and be joined to his wife, and the two shall become one flesh'? [6] So then, they are no longer two but one flesh. Therefore what God has joined together, let not man separate. Matthew 19:4-6

True freedom guarantees every individual to enjoy complete personal liberties as prescribed by God and as stated in the declaration of Independence of the United States:

"That we hold these truths to be self-evident, that all men are created equal, that they are endowed by their Creator with certain unalienable Rights, that among these are Life, Liberty and the pursuit of happiness. That to secure these rights, Governments are instituted among Men, deriving their just powers from the consent of the governed."

Free-enterprise environment safeguards individual citizens' right to produce, innovate and start up new businesses.

God's mandate to us is to have dominion and to occupy until He comes.

[28] Then God blessed them, and God said to them, "Be fruitful and multiply; fill the earth and subdue it; have dominion over the fish of the sea, over the birds of the air, and over every living thing that moves on the earth." Genesis 1:28

But God did not give us any mandate to exercise dominion on fellow human beings!

As Christians, we are the determinants of how much of God's dominion, power and influence operate within our nations.

We are to enter most solemn, enduring and sacred commitments with God to see His intervention in the day-to-day life of our nations. These commitments are also known as covenants and they are always accompanied with terms and conditions.

Fulfilling the terms of the commitments always bring a blessing because God is always a covenant keeper. On the other hand breaking the terms will bring a curse on our lives, nations and future generations. (Deuteronomy 28)

[14] If My people who are called by My name will humble themselves, and pray and seek My face, and turn from their wicked ways, then I will hear from heaven, and will forgive their sin and heal their land. 2 Chronicles 7:14

It can take just a single man or woman to "stand in the gap" between God's judgment and an entire nation.

The people of the land have used oppressions, committed robbery, and mistreated the poor and needy; and they wrongfully oppress the stranger. [30] "So I sought for a man among them who would make a wall, and stand in the gap before Me on behalf of the land, that I should not destroy it; but I found no one. Ezekiel 22:29-30

Ideologies of leaders fill the political vacuum

The creation of apartheid in South Africa is yet another demonstrated fact that the faith and beliefs of those that do govern permeate into the body politic and fills the vacuum.

Their belief system becomes the basis upon which certain laws with profound multi-generational implications are passed.

In the 20th Century, several Christian denominations in South Africa overtly promoted racial divisions based on the political philosophy of apartheid.

Apartheid means "separateness".

The Christian faith became a powerful influence in South Africa and a means of uniting a large number of people.

When the Afrikaner Nationalist party took over the reign of power in 1948, an Act of law was introduced in South Africa that decreed that moving forward, blacks, Indians and Coloreds, would be "separated" from whites, giving favor and supremacy to whites.

Strict segregation orders were enforced forbidding non-whites equal access and rights economically and at the same time denying them similar access to social and educational amenities, and public accommodations as whites.

Many homes of blacks were confiscated and given to whites while blacks were forced to live in extremely poor conditions and the voices of protest were silenced.

When they protest, they were met with very violent backlash.

The white dominated Dutch Reformed Church (DRC became known as the "Official Religion" of the Afrikaner Nationalist party and supported apartheid, "arguing" from the Bible that:

"God 'deliberately divided people into different races' – the whites being superior to blacks and that means people are only spiritually equal, but not physically equal. That South Africa's apartheid laws were God's Will and that Races should be kept apart. Whites should have better opportunities as they heed God's 'favor'."

"Mixed marriages and relationships were discouraged so that races remained 'pure' and that God is the 'Great Divider' supported by Genesis Chapter 1 in the Bible, in that, God divides everything into separate categories - white is divided from black and meant to be separate."

By the 1990's the Dutch Reformed Church of South Africa had more than 3 million members through its four main branches.

In 1994, South Africa held its first ever-democratic elections and the late Nelson Mandela became the first black president.

The new government set up the Truth and Reconciliation Commission to redress the injustices committed under apartheid.

Anglican Bishop and Nobel Peace Prize laureate
Desmond Tutu chaired the commission.

The Commission summed up the Church's
involvement in apartheid as follows:

"Some of the major Christian churches gave their
blessing to the system of apartheid. And many of its
early proponents prided themselves in being
Christians.

Indeed, the system of apartheid was regarded as
stemming from the mission of the
Church...Religious communities also suffered under
apartheid, their activities were disrupted, their
leaders persecuted, their land taken away.

Churches, mosques, synagogues and temples –
often divided amongst themselves – spawned many
of apartheid's strongest foes, motivated by values
and norms coming from their particular faith
traditions."

The Dutch Reformed Church arrived in South
Africa in the 17th Century from the Netherlands.

John Calvin's teaching of "predestination" became
entrenched in Europe and the governing body of the
Dutch Reformed Church adopted Calvin's teachings
and declared that their church had become "the
community of the elect" in 1619 and was granted
recognition as the official state religion in 1651.

In 1652, Jan Van Reebeck, working for the Dutch East India company, an extension of the state in Southern Africa established the first Dutch Reformed Church at the Cape of Good Hope, and by so doing transplanting their Dutch Reformed theology to the African continent.

John Calvin was born in Noyon, France in1509, to a lawyer layman who served as an administrator of the local Catholic cathedral and had encouraged his son to study to become a Catholic priest.

John was a brilliant Reformation theologian, with views contrary to those of the Roman Catholic Church and Reformer Martin Luther.

He ignited a movement that revolutionized Church doctrine, which became known as Calvinism, in Europe, America, and ultimately the rest of the world.

Calvinism teaches predestination that God divides humanity into two groups:

The Elect, who will be saved and ultimately go to heaven and the damned, who will spend eternity in hell and that Jesus Christ died only for the sins of the Elect instead of dying for the sins of everyone, a doctrine known as Limited Atonement or Particular Redemption.

Calvin also taught the doctrine of Irresistible Grace, that the Elect couldn't resist God's call to salvation upon them.

He also taught what he called the doctrine of Perseverance of the Saints "once saved, always saved" and that no one could lose their salvation, also known as the eternal security.

He also believed that when God began the process of sanctification on a person, God would keep at it until that person went to heaven.

By the 1800s, Europe had evolved and was softening from Calvinism.

It was engulfed in liberal Religious trends but the Dutch Reformed Church in South Africa resisted this liberal stance and the rift resulted in the church breaking its ties away from the Netherlands' control.

Like many mainline Christian churches, the Dutch Reformed Churches also believe that God is eternal, infinite, wise and just and the creator of the Universe, that "He has planned the fate of each individual on earth;

The 'chosen' are saved as long as they adhere to the Church's teaching." They also believe that the Bible, both the New and Old Testaments, is the final authority on religious matters.

The history of the DRC has been very much bound with the politics of the Afrikaner community of South Africa.

The church supported the system of apartheid, which institutionalized separation and stratification of the people of South Africa according to race.

The social segregation of black, colored and white people was reflected in the establishment of churches of these three groups.

As Africans and people of mixed race converted and joined the church, the founding Afrikaner membership of the DRC debated the dilemma of racial integration within the church and pressure mounted for racially separate congregations.

Black members also demanded for their own congregations as a result of racially based ill treatment.

In 1881, a separate DRC church for people of mixed race was formed and by 1910, the black South Africans made up ten percent of the DRC's total membership and in response to that, the Dutch Reformed Church -Africa was created.

The Dutch Reformed Church-Africa began to spread into Africa's hinterland taking root in nations like Zambia and Malawi.

My late dad and most members of my extended family are members of the Dutch Reformed Church in Zambia.

An Indian Dutch Reformed Church was only established in 1951.

The Dutch Reform Church was the most powerful religious institution in South Africa and most of the nation's Presidents and Prime Ministers during the apartheid years were members.

The Church said it hoped to re-unite the Dutch Reformed white, black and mixed-race sister churches which were separated decades ago, with white churches and white congregations still controlling huge amounts of land and wealth.

It was for these reasons the DRC was expelled from the World Council of Churches in the early 1980s for its support of apartheid.

1986 the church showed its "repentance" by reaching out to all members of all racial groups to pray under one umbrella, thus making history by welcoming black people back in the church.

Speaking on behalf of the Church, The Reverend Swanerpoel confessed to great wrongs committed in the past and said that the Dutch Reformed Church was guilty of spiritual and structural injustices under apartheid.

Not everyone was happy with that apology; many observers felt that a great opportunity had been missed because the DRC authorities made no mention of restitution for past wrong doings.

Many people who came before the Truth Commission confessed to gross human rights violations such as murder and abduction.

They cited the church as the spiritual inspiration for their gruesome work in support of the former apartheid regime.

In spite of the end of apartheid, racial divides still exists within the DRC.

In 1996, the DRC had 1 288 837 White members, the Uniting Reformed Church (mainly Colored had 1 216 252 members, and the Reformed Church in Africa (mainly Indian had 2 386 members.

Followers of the Hindu religion comprise seventy percent of the one million South African Indians.

The most heralded political activist of the Hindu faith is Mohandas Mahatma Gandhi, who came from India to South Africa in 1893.

Gandhi's political consciousness began after being forced off a train for refusing to sit in racially segregated seating.

He played a prominent role in the struggles for Indian rights in South Africa through his advocacy and leadership in launching passive resistance campaigns in 1906 known as the Satyagraha "insistence on truth" campaigns.

Gandhi's philosophy and political activism have influenced civil rights activists throughout the world.

Satyagraha influenced Nelson Mandela's struggle against Apartheid in South Africa and Dr. Martin King Jr.' s campaigns during the civil rights movement in the United States.

The Dutch Reformed Church, which supported the system of racial segregation in the country, offered an apology and acknowledged apartheid as a sin, two years after the release of Nelson Mandela from prison.

CHAPTER 8

CHRISTIANS AND POLITICS

In simple terms, politics deals with the governance and formation of public policies of a county, State or nation for the preservation of peace, security, administration of resources, and its prosperity.

It also facilitates commerce where its citizens can freely trade in goods and services.

Politics are exercised within the realm of State government, an entity created by God just as the individual, the family, and the Church.

Some Christians genuinely call politics into question, not because it's an illegitimate sphere of

Christian activity, but because it has become a fundamental activity-making partisan politics a source of conflict and strife.

Politics is never meant to save mankind because it has no transforming power that the Gospel of Jesus Christ has.

As Christians, we have been called to avoid worldliness but not the world.

Therefore, there is no escape from the rule of other men who hold political office but by what standard or world-view should these rulers do so?

We can either submit to God's standard of rule, or we risk being ruled by these men in politics who imitate God.

We are to live in the world but not by the world's "Babylonian" system.

The Bible does not support the notion that Christians should abandon the world. To the contrary, we ought to be the salt and the light.

[13] "You are the salt of the earth; but if the salt loses its flavor, how shall it be seasoned? It is then good for nothing but to be thrown out and trampled underfoot by a hill cannot be hidden. [15] Nor do they light a lamp and put it under a basket, but on a lamp stand, and it gives light to all *who are* in the house. [16] Let your light so shine before men, that they may see your good works and glorify your Father in heaven. Matthew 5:13-16

Salt is useless unless it's added to tasteless food as a seasoning. Salt is useless until it is applied to a potentially decaying material for preservation. Light is not needed unless there is darkness.

Christians do not live in the confines of Church buildings.

Like everyone else, we also live in the real world and the decisions made by the politicians also affect our lives.

The government determines, among many other things, what and how much taxes we pay, what is taught and where our children attend school, the quality of the social services we get, and whether or not we are allowed to live with a free conscience and the exercise of our faith.

As Christians, we cannot serve two masters. We cannot have one standard of ethics in church and a different one in the public square.

[24] "No one can serve two masters; for either he will hate the one and love the other, or else he will be loyal to the one and despise the other. You cannot serve God and mammon. Matthew 6:24

[20] Woe to those who call evil good, and good evil; [Who] put darkness for light, and light for darkness; Who put bitter for sweet, and sweet for bitter!
Isaiah 5:20

Two masters are likely to give conflicting ideas and may both be wrong.

[3] Can two walk together, unless they are agreed?

Amos 3:3

Our task as believers of Christ is to subject ourselves to a leader that gives righteous orders and

122

the Scriptures give us the definition of what is righteous.

To argue on the basis of ethics is to argue on the basis of righteousness.

Passing any one given law hurts some people and benefits others. If the same law were not passed, it would reverse the victims and the beneficiaries.

Therefore, to any law passed, there will always be victims and beneficiaries.

And the Church of Jesus Christ ought to be assertive enough to be the victors and not the victims of such laws within the democratic process.

For example, the early Church was at odds with the Roman Empire and the Empire's Jewish officers.

The early Christians were accused of "turning the world upside down".

17 Now when they had passed through Amphipolis and Apollonia, they came to Thessalonica, where there was a synagogue of the Jews. [2] Then Paul, as his custom was, went in to them, and for three Sabbaths reasoned with them from the Scriptures, [3] explaining and demonstrating that the Christ had to suffer and rise again from the dead, and *saying,* "This Jesus whom I preach to you is the Christ." [4] And some of them were persuaded; and a great multitude of the devout Greeks, and not a few of the leading women, joined Paul and Silas.

[5] But the Jews who were not persuaded, becoming envious, took some of the evil men from the marketplace, and gathering a mob, set all the city in an uproar and attacked the house of Jason, and sought to bring them out to the people. [6] But when they did not find them, they dragged Jason and some brethren to the rulers of the city, crying out, "These who have turned the world upside down have come here too. Acts 17: 1-6

Early Christianity challenged and changed the culture of a godless and humanistic way of living.

The early Christians were accused of obeying another King apart from Caesar.

…And these are all acting contrary to the decrees of Caesar, saying there is another king—Jesus. Acts 17:7

In their minds, it was Caesar or Christ, the State or the Kingdom.

If Christians will not transform politics, who will?

The continued absence of a critical mass of Christians of good character and other people of moral conscience in key positions of influence makes the corruption in politics even more pronounced.

Fundamental issues of governance are ethical and the Bible is not neutral on matters of good governance, righteousness, and justice.

Christians who choose neutrality ought to be the exception.

God's throne is firmly anchored on the foundation of Righteousness and justice.

"Righteousness and justice are the foundation of Your throne; Mercy and truth go before Your face."
Psalm 89:14

World events are moving at a very rapid pace and the society, as we know it has fast changed.

At this crossroads the Christian, in general, has two stark choices to make- either rediscover the unambiguous truths of God's word, spiritual authority and leadership influence or be part of the prevailing political correctness that disregards or "re-interprets" God's timeless word to fit popular and contemporary opinion.

The core mission of the Church in Matthew 28:18-20 and Acts 1:4-6 has not antiquated.

We are expected to be steadfast and bold in truth even when our stand is relegated to a minority opinion.

The wicked flee when no one pursues, But the righteous are bold as a lion. Proverbs 28:1

Politics in many parts of the world has overtly become more liberal and the Church's response, in general, has been one of political correctness.

The Evangelical Church, in general, has either conformed to the status quo by backing down on the eternal truths of God's word that govern our conduct and response in the public square or has found a place of convenience for fear of misunderstanding and risk being labeled as religious extremists.

This book is about re-iterating the unequivocal truths about what the Bible teaches on our role as Christians in the public square and to undress the long-held legend about the separation of God and the State- an entity also created by God.

The Church and the State are two distinct institutions, both created by God, and ought to administratively run as separate entities.

But can God and His word be separated from the affairs of the State?

For example, many world leaders take their oath of office by swearing on the Bible or by using a religious book that informs their belief system.

In the United Kingdom, Members of Parliament, including Prime Ministers, can choose to swear on either the New Testament, the Old Testament (in English or Hebrew, the Welsh Bible, the Gaelic Bible, the Koran, or the Granth.

Others are also free to take an affirmation.

Most of the Presidents of the United States have taken the sacred oath of office by swearing on the Bible, as an acknowledgment that fundamental issues of governance require a clear and clean conscience before God and that the word of God is the mirror on issues of good governance, righteousness, and justice.

How is it that the substance in the Bible is disregarded, seen as inconsequential and separate in the process of governing?

In the present dispensation of political correctness, both the Christians and the non-Christians shy away from the idea that the Bible is the blueprint for building strong nations based on fairness or that the current state of affairs is redeemable.

The Word of God is sufficient. It gives us instructions on all we need, including our response, conduct, and position in the realm of leading the affairs of nations.

This is also an awakening the docile church fraternity, at large, to rise and take back its lost ground, spiritual authority and leadership influence in order to establish God's Kingdom here on earth.

We can rest in this eternal fact. We have not been called to build "our own" churches and ministries. The mission is Jesus Christ's and we are simply His

Ambassadors or representatives on earth.

Jesus Christ is building His Church regardless of the external circumstances.

The human race is confronted with pressing needs socially, economically, politically, and religiously.

An evident decline in the moral fiber of society can readily be seen by the assault on marriage and family breakdown, increased drug abuse, illicit and perverted sex, corruption, political confusion and violence, chronic poverty and a rise in religious segmentation, tribalism, and cults.

A good portion of the world's population is still victim to this diabolical condition, worse still it dies to an eternity without Christ.

If the Lord Jesus Christ comes sooner than later, our generation will be justified not to address these concerns.

The gospel call to evangelism must continue with unwavering intensity.

Pastoral care to the needy and sacraments of marriage, child dedication, baptisms and holy communion must continue to foster fellowship and oneness as the family of God on earth.

However, the Church must now give prophetic direction and apostolic establishment as well.

128

³ If the foundations are destroyed, What can the righteous do? Psalms 11:3

And where prophetic vision lacks, people cast off restraint.

¹⁸ Where *there is* no revelation, the people cast off restraint; But happy *is* he who keeps the law. Proverbs 29:18

The Church is the channel through which the God solution must come.

The Church is the agent of change to a dying world. Jesus said:

¹⁰ I am come that they might have life and that they might have it more abundantly. John 10:10

The God kind of life is overflowing, far up and above just an ordinary existence.

His life changes us not only spiritually but in every other realm of our existence, namely: physical, social, economical, cultural and political.

The same transforming power of God's word that sees masses come to Christ, remove and destroy spiritual and physical bondage can now also be trusted to transform economically and politically.

[17] then you say in your heart, 'My power and the might of my hand have gained me this wealth.' [18] "And you shall remember the LORD your God, for *it is* He who gives you power to get wealth, that He may establish His covenant which He swore to your fathers, as *it is* this day. [19] Then it shall be, if you by any means forget the LORD your God, and follow other gods, and serve them and worship them, I testify against you this day that you shall surely perish. Deuteronomy 8: 17-19

God is raising men and women who will seek after His unique plan and purpose for our generation.

A fresh understanding and teaching of God's word are needed to bring true and comprehensive freedom to literally billions of people across the earth.

The Church is a mirror and reflection of any given society. The failures, double standards and mediocrity of the Church in any given area will be reflected in a corresponding deficiency in that society.

As Christians, we should affirm our God given right and privilege, to participate without reservation in shaping our nations politically.

Politics remains one of the major frontiers to be influenced by Biblical truth.

Time is now when God's people everywhere should rise and become relevant and significant.

Christians need not shy away from politics even if they are a "full contact sport" and the partisan jostling for power can be "dirty".

If not the Christians, then who else should possess the moral clarity and integrity to do what is right and just in politics?

As Christians, we are required to redeem or "buy back" politics and the civil sphere of government.

We are never to view politics as the sole or main solution to all our problems.

Our sole involvement in politics is not to replace non-Christians with Christians.

Our goal is to be the salt and the light, to influence and build a civil government based on Biblical principles.

We are to lead and not follow, be the head and not the tail, "intimidators" and not the intimidated, victors and not victims of life's circumstances.

Whatever profession or calling you may be: lawyer, businessman, miner, farmer, politician, preacher, engineer, medical doctor or nurse, police officer, teacher or student, your perception of politics needs to be challenged and changed, and above all, provoked into becoming proactive in your Christian experience.

Some Christians contend that if enough people are born again, the broader culture will change automatically.

However, that can only be possible when they hold key and strategic positions in every area of life, including politics.

Salt must penetrate and mix well with your food to have a good and even taste.

Christians are to be relevant in all spheres of life including the institutions of education, business, law, media, sports, and politics.

Jesus Himself said we are to be shrewd.

[8] So the master commended the unjust steward because he had dealt shrewdly. For the sons of this world are shrewder in their generation than the sons of light. Luke16: 8

In some circles, Christianity is meant to embrace the spiritual dimension of man only.

Christians have been taught how they can get to heaven but not how to successfully live by the principles of God's word here on earth and have, therefore, become "too heavenly minded and no earthly good!"

Christians were taught not to excel in their education because it was "worldly".

132

They were discouraged from entering the business sector because they would "love money more than God".

Poverty was a symbol of "humility" and political involvement in whatever capacity was declared out of bounds for the Church fraternity.

As a result, the Church lost its ground in the public square and is now only playing defense. We need to play to catch up and start scoring again.

There should be no conflict between proselytizing and social responsibility, and if anything, our faith without good deeds is dead.

14 What does it profit, my brethren, if someone says he has faith but does not have works? Can faith save him? 15 If a brother or sister is naked and destitute of daily food, 16 and one of you says to them, "Depart in peace, be warmed and filled," but you do not give them the things which are needed for the body, what does it profit? 17 Thus also faith by itself, if it does not have works, is dead.18 But someone will say, "You have faith, and I have works." Show me your faith without your works, and I will show you my faith by my works. 19 You believe that there is one God. You do well. Even the demons believe—and tremble! 20 But do you want to know, O foolish man, that faith without works is dead? 21 Was not Abraham our father justified by works when he offered Isaac his son on the altar? 22 Do you see that faith was working together with his works, and by works faith was made perfect? James 2:14-22

The denial of political involvement is the denial of many portions of the Scriptures.

The Bible never condemns political involvement.

In different generations, people took up a political office in line with God's purpose.

Moses was both a spiritual and political leader who led the people of Israel out of four hundred years of bondage in Egypt.

Joseph rose to be the most powerful man in Egypt apart from the Pharaoh.

Esther was strategically placed in the King's palace and she was used to saving her fellow Jews from mass execution.

Debora led her nation to victory in the times of the judges. The prophet Daniel rose to a prominent political position in Babylon.

John the Baptist's death was political after challenging King Herod's adulterous affair.

David was prophet and king (today he would be a prophet and president

Paul calls rulers in State government God's ministers, servants in the political sphere. (Romans 13:4-6

Finally, we have to participate and take our civic responsibility to vote very seriously. The disciples replaced Judas Iscariot by casting a vote, after earnest prayer.

[21] "Therefore, of these men who have accompanied us all the time that the Lord Jesus went in and out among us,

[22] beginning from the baptism of John to that day when He was taken up from us, one of these must become a witness with us of His resurrection." [23] And they proposed two: Joseph called Barsabas, who was surnamed Justus, and Matthias. [24] And they prayed and said, "You, O Lord, who know the hearts of all, show which of these two You have chosen [25] to take part in this ministry and apostleship from which Judas by transgression fell, that he might go to his own place."

[26] And they cast their lots, and the lot fell on Matthias. And he was numbered with the eleven apostles. Acts 1:21-26

[5] O LORD, *You are* the portion of my inheritance and my cup; You maintain my lot.[6] The lines have fallen to me in pleasant *places;* Yes, I have a good inheritance. Psalm 16:6

135

CHAPTER 9

THE SEPARATION OF CHURCH AND STATE

Was America founded as a Christian Nation?

There were many competing interests at the founding of these, the United States of America.

The American constitution was not founded on Christianity, but there were Christian men among the key founding fathers who contended for the establishment of Christian values at the heart of its founding.

The America Church-State calculus has always existed from its founding.

Historically, Christianity has been America's majority religion and the basis for many origins of the national culture.

The United States Constitution does not acknowledge God anywhere. Nowhere is religion mentioned in the United States constitution, except in exclusionary terms.

When the constitution was crafted, the founders specified (in Article 6, section3 that, "no religious test shall ever be required as a qualification to any office or public trust under the United States."

This gave equal citizenship to both believers and non-believers alike, making sure that no religion could make the claim of being the official national religion, such as what had happened in England.

Out of the seven most prominent founding fathers, namely: John Adams, John Jay, James Madison, Benjamin Franklin, Thomas Jefferson, George Washington, and Alexander Hamilton, only John Jay was clearly identified as a Christian.

John Jay believed that "Providence has given to our people the choice of their rulers, and it is the duty as well as the privilege and interest of our Christian nation to select and prefer Christians for their rulers."

John Jay was one of three contributors to the Federalist Papers, along with James Madison and Alexander Hamilton, which helped define American government.

Breaking the Myth of Separation and the Deepening Evangelical Division in American Politics

Jay has not been credited enough for his achievements that extend to virtually every branch of government, on the state, federal and international levels.

He was president of the wartime Continental Congress and served as Secretary of foreign affairs (the equivalent to Secretary of State now after the Revolutionary War ended.

Jay was an essential diplomat whose peace negotiations with England led to the signing of the Treaty of Paris and vastly expanded U.S. territory.

The founders robustly debated amongst themselves, but they agreed on the virtues of Jay.

John Adams praised Jay as being "of more importance than any of the rest of us." Alexander Hamilton turned to Jay first when conceiving the Federalist Papers.

George Washington held Jay in high regard and when it came to forming his original Cabinet, he offered the first position, any position for that matter, for Jay to choose.

Jay chose the Supreme Court and became the first United States Chief Justice.

John Jay was a strong Christian. He served both as vice-president of the American Bible Society from1816-21 and its president from 1821- 27, and he was a member of the American Board of Commissioners for Foreign Missions.

John Jay also believed in the exercise God's moral law in public affairs:

"It appears to me that the gospel not only recognizes the whole moral law, and extends and perfects our knowledge of it, but also enjoins on all mankind the observance of it. Being ordained by a legislator of infinite wisdom and rectitude, and in whom there is "no variableness," it must be free from imperfection, and therefore never has, nor ever will require amendment or alteration. Hence, I conclude that the moral law is exactly the same now that it was before the flood."

The other founders were men of "the enlightenment" and not men of Christianity. They were students of the European Enlightenment.

They were Deists who did not believe the Bible was true. They were rather free thinkers who relied on reason only and not faith.

They believed that the universe has a creator who does not concern himself daily with human affairs and does not communicate with people either by revelation or through sacred writings like the Bible.

They also spoke of the "God of nature" or "Creator" but not necessarily the God of the Bible.

They acknowledged the person of Jesus but denied His divinity.

These founding fathers, however, supported prayer and religious observance, unlike the present day threat of "freethinkers" who do not accommodate dissent.

In 1956, the US Congress adopted "In God We Trust" as the national motto. This was not an attempt to impose religion on the public, but a public recognition of God, just as the original intent of the Christian Founders was.

The phrase "In God We Trust" appeared on the U.S. coins as early as the 1850s.

The motto was placed on United States coins during the Civil War, largely because of increased religious sentiment by advocates for the establishment of a "Christian nation".

Then-Secretary of the Treasury, Salmon P. Chase, received many appeals from devout Christians throughout the country, urging him to recognize the Deity on United States coins.

The first of such appeals came in a letter dated November 13, 1861, written by Rev. M. R. Watkinson, a Minister of the Gospel from Ridleyville, Pennsylvania, and read:

"Dear Sir: You are about to submit your annual report to the Congress respecting the affairs of the national finances.

One fact touching our currency has hitherto been seriously overlooked. I mean the recognition of the Almighty God in some form on our coins.

You are probably a Christian. What if our Republic were not shattered beyond reconstruction? Would not the antiquaries of succeeding centuries rightly reason from our past that we were a heathen nation? What I propose is that instead of the goddess of liberty we shall have next inside the 13 stars a ring inscribed with the words PERPETUAL UNION; within the ring the all seeing eye, crowned with a halo; beneath this eye the American flag, bearing in its field stars equal to the number of the States united; in the folds of the bars the words GOD, LIBERTY, LAW.

This would make a beautiful coin, to which no possible citizen could object. This would relieve us from the ignominy of heathenism. This would place us openly under the Divine protection we have personally claimed. From my hearth, I have felt our national shame in disowning God as not the least of our present national disasters.

To you first, I address a subject that must be agitated."

Following these requests, Secretary Chase instructed James Pollock, then Director of the Mint at Philadelphia, to prepare a motto, in a letter dated November 20, 1861. The letter read in part:

"Dear Sir: No nation can be strong except in the strength of God, or safe except in His defense. The trust of our people in God should be declared on our national coins.

You will cause a device to be prepared without unnecessary delay with a motto expressing in the fewest and tersest words possible this national recognition."

Today, all currency bears the religious motto "In God We Trust". This has become a sore spot for many advocates of the "Separation of Church and State".

Multiple lawsuits have been brought against the motto "In God We Trust", but they have so far yielded no success.

The federal courts have maintained that the phrase doesn't establish a religion.

President Thomas Jefferson invented the phrase "the wall of Separation of Church and State"

What then is the "Separation of Church and State" and does it exist in the American Constitution?

On adoption of the American constitution in 1789, fear came that the national government would either interfere with established religions or create a national Church like what was previously done in England.

The many Federal States petitioned the first Congress to include an amendment to the constitution *prohibiting the national government from funding a single Christian denomination or favor it with legal action.*

The enlightenment believers interpreted this to mean that the newly founded nation would be shielded from Christian extremism that had taken hold of politics in Europe.

The enlightenment age was one of reason and free thought, void of any religious belief.

On the flip side, the pilgrim Christians who had fled religious persecution at the hands of the British Monarchy viewed such a petition as a necessary safeguard to preventing the State from meddling in religious liberties.

"Congress shall make no law respecting an establishment of religion, or prohibiting the free exercise thereof; or abridging the freedom of speech, or of the press; or the right of the people peaceably to assemble, and to petition the Government for a redress of grievances."

The real objective of the first amendment was to prohibit the establishment of a national religion where one religious "sect" might obtain pre-eminence over others.

The phrase "Separation of Church and State" is not in the United States constitution yet it is widely believed to be so by many Americans to date. It has been mistaken for the first amendment.

In the minds of the Christian founding fathers, the separation of Christian values of righteousness and justice from the State was never the intent of the first Amendment.

President Thomas Jefferson first coined this metaphor or phrase "the wall of Separation of Church and State", in his letter to avert some specific demands from the Danbury Baptists on January 1, 1802, with regard to the first amendment.

His purpose in this letter was to tone down the fears of the Danbury, Connecticut Baptists and so he told them that this wall had been erected to protect them.

The phrase was used exclusively to keep *the State out of the church's business, not to keep the church's values out of the state's business.*

The misconception about the "Separation of Church and State" is to purposely separate Christian values from the institutions such as education, Law and politics.

While for administrative purposes the Church and the State should be run as separate institutions, there should not be a wall of separation between Christian values and the State, between God and State Government.

How can the two walk together unless they are agreed? (Amos 3:3)

The separation of Church and State Government meant to block Christian values from influencing public policy is not Biblical. It is a myth that has to be broken.

The fear that the Church will usurp State authority and individual liberties of non-Christians is unfounded.

The Church as an institution should not run the State and vice versa. This concept is not Biblical.

However, individual Christians have both the Biblical and constitutional right to participate in the governance of their nations.

It also does not mean that only Christians run State government. There is no religious test as a qualification to run for any office or public trust under the United States Constitution.

Every individual has a right to participate provided the minimum required standard of leadership is met.

It also does not mean that every individual within the nation is compelled to become a Christian.

Christianity is an act of God's love and it is for "whomsoever believes".

[16] For God so loved the world that He gave His only begotten Son, that whoever believes in Him should not perish but have everlasting life. [17] For God did not send His Son in the world to condemn the world, but that the world through Him might be saved. John 3:16-17

In "Ruler of Nations", Gary DeMar defines Theocracy as God's system of Government, which collectively includes: the individual, the family, the Church, and the State.

It is not the rule of the Church as an institution over State government and neither is it a "tyrannical" rule of God over the nations.

Biblical Theocracy means being ruled and guided by God's principles starting with the individual, then the family, Church and the State. Just as there is a prescribed moral standard for the individual, the family, and the Church, God has a moral standard for civil government as well.

If we believe God rules in every area of life, then that's Biblical Theocracy.

The Greek word for God is "theos" and "kratos" for a rule. From the two words, we derive the English word "theocracy".

Theocracy does not mean the rule of the institutional church. This system would be called Ecclesiocracy.

The Bible is opposed to the rule of the institutional Church on Civil government.

Therefore, the persistent use of the term "Theocracy" to describe a civil government that is run by the institutional church is wrong.

This is an attempt to falsify the Biblical meaning of Theocracy, thereby making it repulsive.

This is the most favorite line of attack used by the enemies of the Church and they have used it to scare Christians into political retreat.

This is Biblical Theocracy; an earthly reflection of what the word of God proclaims has always existed, namely; the rule of God in every area not just in civil government or politics.

Humanists define all of life in terms of politics or view politics as the primary way to make life better.

They have defined Theocracy to mean the Church's rule over politics.

Therefore, when the Humanists paint a picture of Theocracy as tyrannical, they are using a wrong model meant to discredit God's order and structure of Government.

The Bible teaches that every area of life is ruled and guided by God's permanent principles.

God rules everything. He is the creator and final judge. God desires that His perfection be reflected in everything man builds.

God is the ruler within His revealed law- which is His word.

The proper goal of Biblical Theocracy in the family, Church, and State is personal responsibility.

Therefore, Biblical Theocracy destroys the economic, legal and psychological dependence of the masses of people on their elite rulers.

The Establishment of a State-run Church in England

Both political and religious persecution motivated America's Pilgrim Fathers to leave the shores of England to start a new Republic.

These pilgrims also known as the "Puritans" were not satisfied with the reforms introduced after the separation of the Church of England (Anglican from the Catholic Holy See in Rome.

In 1593, the English parliament outlawed independent congregations and attendance of the English church services was made mandatory. But the Puritans across the country defied the order and continued to gather.

They had in mind the establishment of a true Church, free from political interference and a nation whose laws and ethical standards reflected a Biblical foundation.

The English Monarchy, however, viewed the Puritans as traitors, a group of renegades defying the authority of King James I.

The pilgrims believed that they were true Christians and puritans, and they were determined to establish the Christian Church, apart from the State's instituted Church of England, by returning to a scripture-based service.

149

Nevertheless, the King and his agents viewed the Puritans as being both seditious and heretical for their beliefs and they were persecuted.

In 1606, a small renegade congregation began in the village of Scrooby in Nottinghamshire, constantly threatened with imprisonment and execution by the King of England and his agents.

They only held out for three years in this location before they were forced to flee and even their several attempts to relocate and settle in other parts of England failed. They had no option left but to emigrate.

They went to Leiden via Amsterdam in the Netherlands, where their religious views found comfort and were tolerated.

By 1618, the pilgrims decided to move again, this time, motivated by fear of another Spanish Catholic invasion of the Netherlands, which would have threatened their newly found religious freedom again and had economic problems and wanted to preserve their heritage.

They resolved to move and settle in the English colony in North America, hoping that England's King and his agents may find it difficult to apprehend them in this remote outpost called America.

Their trip to America was financed by a group of so-called "merchant adventurers". To reciprocate this good gesture, the group was promised a share of the fruits of the pilgrims' labor in North America.

In the summer of 1620, the pilgrims embarked on the ship Mayflower and by September, they finally left England.

There were 102 passengers on board, of which about half were Puritans.

After a stormy 66-day crossing they dropped anchor off Cape Cod near today's Provincetown, in the State of Massachusetts, on November 11, 1620.

CHAPTER 10

BOTTOM-UP HIERARCHY OF GOVERNMENT

One month after leaving Egypt, the Israelites lined up in front of Moses' tent demanding for justice and conflict resolution.

Exodus 18:19-23:

[19] Listen now to my voice; I will give you counsel, and God will be with you: Stand before God for the people, so that you may bring the difficulties to God. [20] And you shall teach them the statutes and the laws, and show them the way in which they must walk and the work they must do. [21] Moreover you shall select from all the people able men, such as fear God, men of truth, hating covetousness; and place *such* over them *to be* rulers of thousands, rulers of hundreds, rulers of fifties, and rulers of tens. [22] And let them judge the people at all times. Then it will be *that* every great matter they shall bring to you, but every small matter they themselves shall judge. So it will be easier for you, for they will bear *the burden* with you. [23] If you do this thing, and God *so* commands

you, then you will be able to endure, and all this people will also go to their place in peace.

Moses' father-in-Law, Jethro, saw what was happening and suggested that Moses should:

1. Serve as God's representative first, an intermediary between God and the Israelites.

2. Teach the people God's Law, so they can know what to do and govern themselves.

3. Appoint righteous men to serve as judges in an appeals court system. They were to mitigate on the easier conflicts, saving the harder ones for Moses to take before God.

In this, Moses understood that God was the sovereign authority and he needed His help to govern the people.

This was in contrast to Egypt's style of government that the Hebrew slaves had gotten used to for 400 years under slavery.

Pharaoh was a hard slave master, a tyrant who was revered as a god.

God through Jethro, was teaching Moses a new order different to the one that the Hebrew slaves had endured.

God was teaching His people the principles of a bottom-up hierarchy of government with a system of redress through appeal.

Top-bottom Pyramid System of Government

The Tower of Babel was the first example of hierarchical pyramid power. These early builders established a political power to "make a name for themselves" by attempting to supplant the government of God. (Genesis 11:4)

This was an act of defiance by claiming sovereignty and power, and by declaring authority of a thing that is named.

They desired to replace it with a bureaucratic and centralized government with everything being controlled from Babel. (Genesis 2:20, Dan. 1:6,7)

Babel wanted to rule the world. Man's intent was to ascend the tower of power in an attempt to grab control over God's created order by centralizing his domain.

This centralized power was Satan's way. He had also wanted to ascend to heaven and raise his thrown above the stars of God.

For you have said in your heart:
'I will ascend into heaven,
I will exalt my throne above the stars of God;
I will also sit on the mount of the congregation
On the farthest sides of the north;
[14] I will ascend above the heights of the clouds,
I will be like the Most High.' Isaiah 14:13-14

Satan wanted to be what God is and the builders of the tower of Babel also wanted to be what God is.

Because they wanted to consolidate all power into one State, God scattered them.

Now the whole world had one language and a common speech. 2 As people moved eastward, they found a plain in Shinar and settled there.

3 They said to each other, "Come, let's make bricks and bake them thoroughly." They used brick instead of stone, and tar for mortar.

4 Then they said, "Come, let us build ourselves a city, with a tower that reaches to the heavens, so that we may make a name for ourselves; otherwise we will be scattered over the face of the whole earth."

5 But the LORD came down to see the city and the tower the people were building. 6 The LORD said, "If as one people speaking the same language they have begun to do this, then nothing they plan to do will be impossible for them.

7 Come, let us go down and confuse their language so they will not understand each other."

8 So the LORD scattered them from there over all the earth, and they stopped building the city.

9 That is why it was called Babel—because there the LORD confused the language of the whole world. From there the LORD scattered them over the face of the whole earth.

Genesis 11:1-9

From one blood He has made every nation of men.

[26] And He has made from one blood every nation of men

to dwell on all the face of the earth, and has determined their pre-appointed times and the boundaries of their dwellings, [27] so that they should seek the Lord, in the hope that they might grope for Him and find Him, though He is not far from each one of us. Acts 17:26-27

And they sang a new song, saying:

You are worthy to take the scroll,
And to open its seals;
For You were slain,
And have redeemed us to God by Your blood
Out of every tribe and tongue and people and nation, 10
And have made us kings and priests to our God; And we
shall reign on the earth."
Revelation 5:9-10

Secular culture views "government" as a top-down
bureaucracy that controls everything in society and
man becomes the central being in control.

It is on this basis that the so-called "New World
Order" is meant to function as a top-down system
of world rule. This new order proposes a new
period of history, which will bring about a major
change in the balance of world power led by groups
of elitists bent on ruling through a single worldwide
system of government.

The bait for this "New World Order" lays in its
attractive proposals to free the world of ills such as
wars and political strife, while promising to
eradicate poverty, disease, and hunger.

It also promises to meet the needs and hopes of all
mankind through worldwide peace.

This phenomenon is also called the "era of
globalization," which will supposedly do away
with the need for diverse world governments.

This will be accomplished by the installation of a one-world political system or body by eliminating all lines and borders demarcating the nation states.

The goal is to effect change through tolerance by the promotion and acceptance of other cultures, values, and ideologies. The ultimate goal is the creation of a one-world rule through oneness by the use of a single worldwide currency, and a political and religious system that define uniform morals.

By so doing, the new-world order will achieve worldwide peace, the absence of war, and the elimination of all political unrest.

But the word of God declares:

Why do the nations rage,
And the people plot a vain thing?

[2] The kings of the earth set themselves,
And the rulers take counsel together,
Against the Lord and against His Anointed, *saying,*

[3] "Let us break Their bonds in pieces
And cast away Their cords from us. Psalm 2:1-3

The Bible teaches that the word "government" is a general term for self, family, church and civil governments. The Bible rejects the notion of "government" being a top-down bureaucracy. Instead, it teaches that it is bottom-up starting with individual responsibility.

Decentralized System Government

In contrast to the pyramid system, God's system of political power is decentralized and plural in nature. No single institution has been established to bring about social order.

There is an intellectual and spiritual war going on, a war between rival views of God, man, law and the order of society. On one hand is Christianity, which advocates plural governments, institutional independence and the Bible, which is the moral code of God and the source of checks and balances. On the other is the anti-Christian view. It holds a completely different viewpoint of the world. It believes that man, and not God, is the sovereign agent of all authority and over the institutions such as the State, Education, Science, and Law.

God is the ultimate authority who governs all things.

(Jeremiah 27:5, Proverbs 8:15

God is the independent and unlimited governing authority while man, Church, and human institutions are limited governing authorities. (Exodus 18, Romans 13:1-4)

Individual Christians exercise self-discipline or self-control, parents exercise authority over their children, wives are submissive, in love, to their husbands, employers over employees, teachers over students, elders or bishops over church members, and civil servants over citizens.

Under God, there is one law and one lawgiver. He has created plural authorities to which we must all submit.

This system of government makes it very hard for a single individual to dominate. No one given authority can claim the right to overshadow other established authorities except God.

Ultimately, all delegated authorities are responsible to God for legitimacy.

Corruption and dictatorship sets in when structures from the individual, family, church and civil authorities breakdown.

All authority then tends to rest in one institution, usually the State.

Functional and diverse authority structures cannot arise by themselves.

They come about when the individual assumes personal responsibility under God, transforms his family and working with other like-minded individuals transforms his school, church, local and national civil governments.

The State has limited jurisdiction and competence. It offers temporal punishment for criminal acts but it's not man's answer for sin.

The welfare State grows in proportion to the failure of individuals, families, businesses, schools and churches.

The people in Gideon's generation looked to a fellow man as the solution to all their problems.

[22] The Israelites said to Gideon, "Rule over us—you, your son and your grandson—because you have saved us from the hand of Midian." [23] But Gideon told them, "I will not rule over you, nor will my son rule over you. The LORD will rule over you. Judges 8:22-23, NIV

They felt that if they just chose a powerful king to rule over them, their problems would be solved.

When Abimelech murdered his opposition he promised the people security if they would only follow him. This opened the door to a tyrant.

Then Abimelech the son of Jerubbaal went to Shechem, to his mother's brothers, and spoke with them and with all the family of the house of his mother's father, saying,

[2] "Please speak in the hearing of all the men of Shechem: 'Which is better for you, that all seventy of the sons of Jerubbaal reign over you, or that one reign over you?' Remember that I *am* your own flesh and bone."

[3] And his mother's brothers spoke all these words concerning him in the hearing of all the men of Shechem; and their heart was inclined to follow Abimelech, for they said, "He is our brother." [4] So they gave him seventy *shekels* of silver from the temple of Baal-Berith, with which Abimelech hired worthless and reckless men; and they followed him. [5] Then he went to his father's house at Ophrah and killed his brothers, the seventy sons of Jerubbaal, on one stone. But Jotham the youngest son of Jerubbaal was left, because he hid himself. [6] And all the men of Shechem gathered together, all of Beth Millo, and they went and made Abimelech king beside the terebinth tree at the pillar that *was* in Shechem. Judges 9:1-6

When there was a lack of holiness (Judges 14-16) and priesthood (1 Samuel 2:12-17, 22-36), the people turned to the State for salvation. (1 Samuel 8)

CHAPTER 11

GOD'S JUDGMENT OF NATIONS

God not only judges individuals but collective nations also.

As individuals, we will all inescapably face the judgment seat of God.

[27] Just as people are destined to die once, and after that to face judgment, [28] so Christ was sacrificed once to take away the sins of many; and he will appear a second time, not to bear sin, but to bring salvation to those who are waiting for him. Hebrews 9:27-28, NIV

God has also promised that He will judge the nations.

[6] And the angels who did not keep their proper domain, but left their own abode, He has reserved in everlasting chains under darkness for the judgment of the great day;

[7] as Sodom and Gomorrah, and the cities around them in a similar manner to these, having given themselves over to sexual immorality and gone after strange flesh, are set forth as an example, suffering the vengeance of eternal fire." Jude 1:5-7

[30] Truly, these times of ignorance God overlooked, but now commands all men everywhere to repent, [31] because

He has appointed a day on which He will judge the world in righteousness by the Man whom He has ordained. He has given assurance of this to all by raising Him from the dead." Acts 17:30-31

Beloved, I now write to you this second epistle (in *both of* which I stir up your pure minds by way of reminder), [2] that you may be mindful of the words which were spoken before by the holy prophets, and of the commandment of us, the apostles of the Lord and Savior, [3] knowing this first: that scoffers will come in the last days, walking according to their own lusts, [4] and saying, "Where is the promise of His coming? For since the fathers fell asleep, all things continue as *they were* from the beginning of creation." [5] For this they willfully forget: that by the word of God the heavens were of old, and the earth standing out of water and in the water, [6] by which the world *that* then existed perished, being flooded with water. [7] But the heavens and the earth *which* are now preserved by the same word, are reserved for fire until the day of judgment and perdition of ungodly men.[8] But, beloved, do not forget this one thing, that with the Lord one day *is* as a thousand years, and a thousand years as one day. [9] The Lord is not slack concerning *His* promise, as some count slackness, but is longsuffering toward us not willing that any should perish but that all should come to repentance.[10] But the day of the Lord will come as a thief in the night, in which the heavens will pass away with a great noise, and the elements will melt with fervent heat; both the earth and the works that are in it will be burned up. 2 Peter 3:1-10

When Jesus sent out His twelve Disciples, He reminded them of the Judgment day to come.

[11] "Now whatever city or town you enter, inquire who in it is worthy, and stay there till you go out. [12] And when you go into a household, greet it. [13] If the household is worthy, let your peace come upon it. But if it is not worthy, let your peace return to you. [14] And whoever will not receive you nor hear your words, when you depart from that house or city, shake off the dust from your feet. [15] Assuredly, I say to you, it will be more tolerable for the land of Sodom and Gomorrah in the day of judgment than for that city! Matthew 10:11-15

Some have contended that God only judged entire nations during the Old Covenant times and not in the New Testament.

But the "almighty Roman empire" crumbled in the era of the Church three centuries after the cross, although its downfall was prophesied earlier through King Nebuchadnezzar's dream.

Daniel interpreted the King's dream that the gold stood for King Nebuchadnezzar's Babylon and him as the greatest King.

[31] "You, O king, were watching; and behold, a great image! This great image, whose splendor *was* excellent, stood before you; and its form *was* awesome. [32] This image's head *was* of fine gold, its chest and arms of silver, its belly and thighs of bronze, [33] its legs of iron, its feet partly of iron and partly of clay. [34] You watched while a stone was cut out without hands, which struck the image on its feet of iron and clay, and broke them in pieces. [35] Then the iron, the clay, the bronze, the silver, and the gold were crushed together, and became like chaff from the summer threshing floors; the wind carried them away so that no trace of them was found. And the

stone that struck the image became a great mountain and filled the whole earth. Daniel 2:31-35

There would be three other Kingdoms after his and the fourth would be the Iron Empire, Rome.

The Roman Empire would break all other kingdoms and consolidate into clay and iron.

[40] And the fourth kingdom shall be as strong as iron, inasmuch as iron breaks in pieces and shatters everything; and like iron that crushes, *that kingdom* will break in pieces and crush all the others. [41] Whereas you saw the feet and toes, partly of potter's clay and partly of iron, the kingdom shall be divided; yet the strength of the iron shall be in it, just as you saw the iron mixed with ceramic clay. [42] And *as* the toes of the feet *were* partly of iron and partly of clay, *so* the kingdom shall be partly strong and partly fragile. [43] As you saw iron mixed with ceramic clay, they will mingle with the seed of men; but they will not adhere to one another, just as iron does not mix with clay. Daniel 2: 40-42

Christ established His kingdom as manifested through, but not limited to the Church, during the Roman Empire.

[44] And in the days of these kings the God of heaven will set up a kingdom which shall never be destroyed; and the kingdom shall not be left to other people; it shall break in pieces and consume all these kingdoms, and it shall stand forever. [45] Inasmuch as you saw that the stone was cut out of the mountain without hands, and that it broke in pieces the iron, the bronze, the clay, the silver, and the gold—the great God has made known to the king

what will come to pass after this. The dream is certain, and its interpretation is sure." Daniel 2: 44-45

God also refers to His people on earth collectively, as a Holy nation.

[9] But you *are* a chosen generation, a royal priesthood, a holy nation, His own special people, that you may proclaim the praises of Him who called you out of darkness into His marvelous light. 1Peter 2:9

God first destroyed the earth, in Noah's generation.

Then the LORD said to Noah, "Come into the ark, you and all your household, because I have seen *that* you *are* righteous before Me in this generation. [2] You shall take with you seven each of every clean animal, a male and his female; two each of animals that *are* unclean, a male and his female; [3] also seven each of birds of the air, male and female, to keep the species alive on the face of all the earth. [4] For after seven more days I will cause it to rain on the earth forty days and forty nights, and I will destroy from the face of the earth all living things that I have made." [5] And Noah did according to all that the LORD commanded him. [6] Noah *was* six hundred years old when the floodwaters were on the earth. Genesis 7:1-6

After man attempted to build the Tower of Babel to reach Heaven, in an act of defiance, God judged their actions by destroying the Tower, divided them linguistically, and scattered mankind across the face of the earth.

Mankind was divided into independent, sovereign, and language-based nations. (Genesis 11:1-9

God also judged Sodom and Gomorrah in the land of Canaan.

[20] And the LORD said, "Because the outcry against Sodom and Gomorrah is great, and because their sin is very grave, [21] I will go down now and see whether they have done altogether according to the outcry against it that has come to Me; and if not, I will know." Genesis 18:20-21

These were very prosperous cities. Abraham's Nephew Lot turned to Sodom and Gomorrah when his uncle offered him a place of his choice in Canaan.

[10] And Lot lifted his eyes and saw all the plain of Jordan, that it *was* well watered everywhere (before the Lord destroyed Sodom and Gomorrah like the garden of the Lord, like the land of Egypt as you go toward Zoar. Genesis 13:10

For the sake of his Nephew Lot, Abraham bargained with God to spare the cities from destruction.

[22] Then the men turned away from there and went toward Sodom, but Abraham still stood before the LORD. [23] And Abraham came near and said, "Would You also destroy the righteous with the wicked? [24] Suppose there were fifty righteous within the city; would You also destroy the place and not spare *it* for the fifty righteous that were

in it? [25] Far be it from You to do such a thing as this, to slay the righteous with the wicked, so that the righteous should be as the wicked; far be it from You! Shall not the Judge of all the earth do right?"[26] So the LORD said, "If I find in Sodom fifty righteous within the city, then I will spare all the place for their sakes."[27] Then Abraham answered and said, "Indeed now, I who *am but* dust and ashes have taken it upon myself to speak to the Lord: [28] Suppose there were five less than the fifty righteous; would You destroy all of the city for *lack of* five?" So He said, "If I find there forty-five, I will not destroy *it.*"[29] And he spoke to Him yet again and said, "Suppose there should be forty found there?" So He said, "I will not do *it* for the sake of forty."[30] Then he said, "Let not the Lord be angry, and I will speak: Suppose thirty should be found there?" So He said, "I will not do *it* if I find thirty there."[31] And he said, "Indeed now, I have taken it upon myself to speak to the Lord: Suppose twenty should be found there?" So He said, "I will not destroy *it* for the sake of twenty."[32] Then he said, "Let not the Lord be angry, and I will speak but once more: Suppose ten should be found there?" And He said, "I will not destroy *it* for the sake of ten." Genesis 18:22-32

Only Lot, his wife, and two daughters left the city and the rest were destroyed by fire and Brimstone. (Genesis 19:14)

CHAPTER 12

MORAL CONSCIENCE GOVERNS A NATION'S CORE VALUES

Morality and integrity matter. Leaders of nations have a moral responsibility to uphold righteous behavior and equal justice for all.

A tension has always existed between the Church and Civil government on matters of ethics, justice and equitable distribution of goods and services especially toward the poor, weak and the voiceless.

There are several occasions in the Bible where God's prophets demanded moral behavior and justice even from pagan rulers based on God's standard of righteousness.

John confronted Herod about his adulterous affair

John the Baptist was consequently beheaded because he rebuked Herod for his adulterous relationship with his brother's wife.

14 Now King Herod heard of Him, for His name had become well known. And he said, "John the Baptist is risen from the dead, and therefore these powers are at work in him."

15 Others said, "It is Elijah." And others said, "It is the Prophet, or like one of the prophets."

[16] But when Herod heard, he said, "This is John, whom I beheaded; he has been raised from the dead!" [17] For Herod himself had sent and laid hold of John, and bound him in prison for the sake of Herodias, his brother Philip's wife; for he had married her. [18] Because John had said to Herod, "It is not lawful for you to have your brother's wife." [19] Therefore Herodias held it against him and wanted to kill him, but she could not; [20] for Herod feared John, knowing that he *was* a just and holy man, and he protected him. And when he heard him, he did many things, and heard him gladly. [21] Then an opportune day came when Herod on his birthday gave a feast for his nobles, the high officers, and the chief *men* of Galilee. [22] And when Herodias' daughter herself came in and danced, and pleased Herod and those who sat with him, the king said to the girl, "Ask me whatever you want, and I will give *it* to you." [23] He also swore to her, "Whatever you ask me, I will give you, up to half my kingdom."[24] So she went out and said to her mother,
"What shall I ask?" And she said, "The head of John the Baptist!"[25] Immediately she came in with haste to the king and asked, saying, "I want you to give me at once the head of John the Baptist on a platter."[26] And the king was exceedingly sorry; *yet,* because of the oaths and because of those who sat with him, he did not want to refuse her. [27] Immediately the king sent an executioner and commanded his head to be brought. And he went and beheaded him in prison, [28] brought his head on a platter, and gave it to the girl; and the girl gave it to her mother.

[29] When his disciples heard *of it,* they came and took away his corpse and laid it in a tomb. Mark 6: 14-29

Herod Antipus was a powerful ruler, a Tetrarch who ruled over one-quarter of a Roman province.

John the Baptist rebuked Herod for taking another man's wife, Herodius, who had been married to Herod's half-brother, Phillip. He told Herod that, "It is not lawful for you to have your brother's wife."

Herodius was furious and convinced Herod to arrest John and put an end to the large crowds John the Baptist was attracting.

Herod was Roman and was not a believer. Nonetheless, John the Baptist used the law of God to judge Herod's behavior because he was a civil ruler over his affairs and that of his people the Israelites.

Therefore, it is an unfounded notion that we cannot look to public policy and the behavior of our rulers to reflect God's law and ethics.

[2] When the righteous are in authority, the people rejoice;

But when a wicked *man* rules, the people groan.

Proverbs 29:2

John the Baptist died for righteousness' sake.

[10] Blessed *are* those who are persecuted for righteousness' sake, for theirs is the kingdom of heaven. [11] "Blessed are you when they revile and persecute you, and say all kinds of evil against you falsely for My sake. [12] Rejoice and be exceedingly glad,

for great *is* your reward in heaven, for so they persecuted the prophets who were before you. Matthews 5: 10-12

The Prophet Nathan confronted King David about his adulterous affair

King David had had a moral failure of good judgment. He used his power and influence as King over Israel and committed adultery with Bathsheba, the wife of one of his most trusted soldiers, Uriah.

He then connived to get Uriah intoxicated with wine, so he could sleep with his wife to cover up his transgression because the woman had conceived with the King's child.

But Uriah refused to do so. He was a principled man who refused to lay with his wife when the rest of the men of Israel were at the battlefront defending the nation.

When the plot failed, King David further organized for the killing of Uriah on the battlefront.
God was not pleased with the King's behavior.

He raised the Prophet Nathan, to rebuke the King and announce God's judgment.

Then the Lord sent Nathan to David. And he came to him, and said to him: "There were two men in one city, one rich and the other poor. [2] The rich *man* had exceedingly many flocks and herds. [3] But the poor *man* had nothing, except one little ewe lamb which he had bought and nourished; and it grew up together with him and with his children. It ate of his own food and drank from his own cup and lay in his bosom; and it was like a daughter to him. [4] And a traveler came to the rich man, who refused to take from his own flock and from his own herd to prepare one for the wayfaring man who had come to him; but he took the poor man's lamb and prepared it for the man who had come to him." [5] So David's anger was greatly aroused against the man, and he said to Nathan, "*As* the Lord lives, the man who has done this shall surely die! [6] And he shall restore fourfold for the lamb, because he did this thing and because he had no pity." [7] Then Nathan said to David, "You *are* the man! Thus says the Lord God of Israel: 'I anointed you king over Israel, and I delivered you from the hand of Saul. [8] I gave you your master's house and your master's wives into your keeping, and gave you the house of Israel and Judah. And if *that had been* too little, I also would have given you much more! [9] Why have you despised the commandment of the Lord, to do evil in His sight? You have killed Uriah the Hittite with the sword; you have taken his wife *to be* your wife, and have killed him with the sword of the people of Ammon. [10] Now therefore, the sword shall never depart from your house, because you have despised Me, and have taken the wife of Uriah the Hittite to be your wife.' [11] Thus says the Lord: 'Behold, I will raise up adversity against you from your own house; and I will take your wives before your eyes and give *them* to your neighbor, and he shall lie with your wives in the sight of this sun. [12] For you did *it* secretly, but I will do this thing before all Israel, before the sun.'"

[13] So David said to Nathan, "I have sinned against the Lord." And Nathan said to David, "The Lord also has put away your sin; you shall not die. [14] However,

because by this deed you have given great occasion to the enemies of the Lord to blaspheme, the child also *who is* born to you shall surely die." [15] Then Nathan departed to his house. 2 Samuel 12: 1-14

Moses confronted the tyrant Pharaoh about slavery: "Let My people go"

One of the most intriguing stories of liberation is to be found in the book of Exodus in the Bible. It is the life story of Moses and his people, the Israelites in Egypt.

These were the sons of Israel who went with the Patriarch Jacob to Egypt for refuge, namely:

Rueben, Simeon, Levi and Judah, Issachar, Zebulun and Benjamin, Dan and Nephtali, Gad and Usher, and Joseph who had earlier been sold into slavery by his own brothers.

The Israelites became fruitful and increased numerically in population to the extent that the whole land of Egypt was full of them.

But a new Egyptian King, also called the Pharaoh arose and the descendants of the Israelites or Hebrews, including Joseph who had risen to Prime Minister of Egypt, meant nothing to the new King.

The new Pharaoh plotted on how to subjugate the Israelites. He introduced forced and hard labor and put ruthless slave masters to watch over them.

The more the Egyptians oppressed the Israelites, the more they grew in numbers and spread across Egypt.

The Pharaoh perturbed by this, resorted to even more desperate measures.

He instructed two Hebrew midwives, Shiphrah and Puah, to kill all baby boys born to Hebrew women at delivery and only the baby girls were to live.

But the two Hebrew midwives feared God and instead they let the Hebrew baby boys to live. When asked by the Pharaoh as to why they did not obey his orders, the midwives answered:

Hebrew women are not like Egyptian women; they are vigorous and give birth before the midwives arrive. Exodus 1:9, NIV

God blessed the midwives with families of their own.

A timeless lesson learned is to be careful whom we invite as "midwives" within the confines of our dreams and visions.

Many dreams and visions have been killed right from inception because the people we shared and confided in did not act like the wise Hebrew midwives.

They killed our dreams and vision at birth.

Be careful whom you allow in the confines of the "birth chambers" and give ear to your dreams, vision, career, marriage or family life.

Breaking the Myth of Separation and the Deepening Evangelical Division in American Politics

The Pharaoh did not relent in his effort to eliminate all Hebrew baby boys.

He gave new orders that "Every Hebrew boy that is born you must throw into the Nile, but let every girl live." Exodus1: 22, NIV

Moses was one such Hebrew baby boy who was born during this period of oppression of his people, the Israelites.

Moses' mother saw that he was a fine child and hid him from the fatal wrath of the Pharaoh and his Egyptian subjects.

After three months, she could hide Moses no longer and had to hide him among the reeds of the River Nile in a floating papyrus basket, with tar and pitch coating.

Moses' sister watched him from a distance.

But divine providence was upon Moses' life.

While he lay down among the reeds of the River Nile, Pharaoh's daughter who had gone to bath by the river noticed him.

Moses' basket lay by the reeds and she ordered her female slaves who minded her to fetch it and she felt pity for baby Moses.

As divine favor would have it, Moses' sister stepped up and asked Pharaoh's daughter, "Shall I go and get one of the Hebrew women to nurse the baby for you?" Exodus 2:7, NIV

Pharaoh's daughter was affirmative and the girl went and got Moses' biological mother to nurse her own son and got paid for it by Pharaoh's daughter!

[20] Now to Him who is able to do exceedingly abundantly above all that we ask or think, according to the power that works in us. Ephesians 3:20

After Moses grew older, his mother took him to Pharaoh's daughter and he became her son and she named him Moses, meaning "I drew him out of the water."

Moses grew into his own, and chose to identify with his people the Hebrews, forsaking all the comforts and security of Pharaoh's palace.

[23] By faith Moses, when he was born, was hidden three months by his parents, because they saw *he was* a beautiful child; and they were not afraid of the king's command. [24] By faith Moses, when he became of age, refused to be called the son of Pharaoh's daughter, [25] choosing rather to suffer affliction with the people of God than to enjoy the passing pleasures of sin, [26] esteeming the reproach of Christ greater riches than the treasures in Egypt; for he looked to the reward. Hebrews 11:23-26

One day, Moses went out to visit his fellow Israelites at their site of hard labor. His anger was aroused when he saw an Egyptian beating a Hebrew.

Moses' God given instinct of a liberator kicked in and he killed the Egyptian.

It was his own fellow Hebrew that threatened to expose his crime.

[20] Then, as they came out from Pharaoh, they met Moses and Aaron who stood there to meet them. [21] And they said to them, "Let the LORD look on you and judge, because you have made us abhorrent in the sight of Pharaoh and in the sight of his servants, to put a sword in their hand to kill us." Exodus 5:20-21

Many times, slaves need their tyrant masters in much the same way that tyrants need their slaves; a condition of mutual benefit.

His calling to liberate Israel was premature at this stage.

He would flee from Pharaoh's wrath for this offence into the wilderness for forty years in hiding before the fullness of his calling.

In his place of hiding Moses started a family and he would tend after his father-in-law's flock in the wilderness.

A wilderness is a natural environment that has not been significantly modified by human activity. It can be a serene place without much activity.

There will be seasons in our callings when nothing much seems to be happening but it is God who brings us there.

There are valuable lessons to be learned and our character develops and matures as we wait on God.

These traits are inculcated in our lives when there is an apparent stagnation.

Moses was educated and raised among the very best of Egypt, having been raised in Pharaoh's palace but in the wilderness he tended after livestock.

The wilderness feels like a debasing of our lives but that is where greatness is born. It is a place of conflict between what we ought to be and the meager state the wilderness brings us into. Those that desire greatness must also embrace the wilderness.

In the expanse of time, the Pharaoh died but the reckoning of the children of Israel under the curse of slavery did not subside but instead increased.

 But this time their cry reached God and He remembered the covenant He made with their forefathers.

[24] So God heard their groaning, and God remembered His covenant with Abraham, with Isaac, and with Jacob. [25] And God looked upon the children of Israel, and God acknowledged *them.* Exodus 2: 24-25

After many decades, God miraculously appeared and revealed Himself to Moses in a "burning bush" whilst he tended after livestock and reminded him of his calling to liberate Israel out of Egypt.

[29] For the gifts and the calling of God *are* irrevocable. Romans11: 29

The wilderness can also be a place of revelation and intimacy with God. It would also appear that great commissions by God are birthed in the wilderness.

[7] And the LORD said:

I have surely seen the oppression of My people
who *are* in Egypt, and have heard their cry because of
their taskmasters, for I know their sorrows. [8] So I have
come down to deliver them out of the hand of the
Egyptians, and to bring them up from that land to a good
and large land, to a land flowing with milk and honey, to
the place of the Canaanites and the Hittites and the
Amorites and the Perizzites and the Hivites and the
Jebusites. [9] Now therefore, behold, the cry of the
children of Israel has come to Me, and I have also seen
the oppression with which the Egyptians oppress them.

[10] Come now, therefore, and I will send you to Pharaoh
that you may bring My people, the children of Israel, out
of Egypt. Exodus 3: 7-10

Moses challenged and spoke directly to Pharaoh's
moral conscience.

Moses, in the company of his brother Aaron, went
back to Egypt and boldly declared to the Pharaoh,
Thus says the LORD God of Israel: 'Let My people go,
that they may hold a feast to Me in the wilderness.
Exodus 5:1

Through a series of God's miracles and
interventions on behalf of His people, Moses
liberated the Israelites from Egypt's bondage with a
decisive victory at the Red Sea.

[13] And Moses said to the people, "Do not be afraid.
Standstill, and see the salvation of the LORD, which He
will accomplish for you today. For the Egyptians whom
you see today, you shall see again no more
forever. [14] The LORD will fight for you, and you shall
hold your peace. Exodus 14:13-14

The children of Israel walked on the dry grounds of the Red Sea when the Lord parted the waters for them and the same waters came back onto the Egyptian Army, on their chariots and on their horses and they all perished.

CHAPTER 13

RACE, CHURCH, AND POLITICS IN THE UNITED STATES

Liberation theology deals with social justice and how the poor, minorities, and in some cases people of color, are exploited or oppressed politically and economically. This is the platform of the Christian left.

It is commonplace in many black American churches in the United States and parts of the world where they have experienced such oppression.

The fight by the people of faith to end slavery, Jim Crow segregation and for Civil Rights in the United States, apartheid in South Africa and colonization across the world was based on the belief that all human beings are of equal value before God.

They understood that while God gave us the mandate to subdue the earth, He never gave any man the right to dominate other fellow human beings.
They also knew that all humanity was meant to be free from both spiritual and physical bondage, through Christ's redemption on the cross.

[28] There is neither Jew nor Greek, there is neither slave nor free, there is neither male nor female; for you are all one in Christ Jesus. Galatians 3:28

In 1968, at the National Cathedral in Washington DC during his last Sunday sermon before he was assassinated, the Rev. Dr. Martin Luther King Jr. famously declared that,"We must face the sad fact that at 11 o'clock on Sunday morning when we stand to sing 'In Christ there is no East or West,' we stand in the most segregated hour of America."

Reverend Dr. Martin Luther King Jr., declared that, "Sunday morning is the most segregated hour of Christian America."

As startling as this is, most American congregations are segregated. Nine out of ten congregations in the U.S. comprise a single racial group accounting for more than 80 percent of their membership.

A segregated church does not necessarily imply that its members are racist, and many contemporary churches that are dominated by one racial group weren't formed by racial animosity. Church members may prefer to go to a church with people who look like them or have similar cultural values, language or national origin. People choose churches where they feel comfortable.

By ministering to a Samaritan woman at the well, Jesus demonstrated that true worship, in Spirit and truth, was intrinsically connected to ministry across cultural and racial lines.

The Samaritan woman said to him, "You are a Jew and I am a Samaritan woman. How can you ask me for a drink?" (For Jews do not associate with Samaritans.) 10 Jesus answered her, "If you knew the gift of God and who it is that asks you for a drink, you would have asked him and he would have given you living water." 23 Yet a time is coming and has now come when the true worshipers will worship the Father in the Spirit and in truth, for they are the kind of worshipers the Father seeks. 24 God is spirit, and his worshipers must worship in the Spirit and in truth." John 4: 9, 10, and 23

While rigid ethnic and class divisions characterized the ancient Roman society, the first Christian church, on the other hand, was known for its diversity. *Jews, Gentiles, and Greeks mingled alongside women and slaves, making the early church's diversity one of the reasons it became so popular.*

Modern Day Liberation Theology

The exposure of a modern day type of liberation theology to the rest of America came as a shock when the following utterances were aired on nearly all media outlets:

"We bombed Hiroshima, we bombed Nagasaki, and we nuked far more than the thousands in New York and the Pentagon, and we never batted an eye."

"We have supported state terrorism against the Palestinians and black South Africans, and now we are indignant because the stuff we have done overseas is now brought right back to our own front yards. America's chickens are coming home to roost."

The government gives them the drugs, builds bigger prisons, passes a three-strike law and then wants us to sing 'God Bless America.' No, no, no, God damn America, that's in the Bible for killing innocent people. God damn America for treating our citizens as less than human. God damn America for as long as she acts like she is God and she is supreme."

These were words spoken in sermons that almost jeopardized the presidential aspirations of then-Senator Barack Obama in the historic 2008 presidential elections.

The sermons were not preached by Mr. Obama but by his Pastor of over 20 years. There was no evidence that he was in attendance when these particular sermons were delivered.

 It was Reverend Jeremiah Wright's sermon that almost overshadowed the entire presidential race.

Reverend Wright was the Senior Pastor at Trinity Church of Christ on 95th Street, on the South side of Chicago where Mr. Obama and his family attended church as members.

Reverend Wright also officiated at the marriage of Mr. Obama to his wife Michelle and baptized their two daughters, Malia, and Sasha.

Some of the quotes that became attributed to Reverend Wright were deemed both un-American and un-patriotic.

The question posed was whether or not then-candidate Obama shared the same views as expressed by his pastor while running to become Commander-in-Chief of the United States armed forces.

Consequently, Mr. Obama gave the Philadelphia speech on race in America in order to contain the political backlash.

Mr. Obama's speech on race in the United States became one of the greatest milestones in his bid for the Presidency of the United States.

It highlighted the complex nature of the dynamic of race, church, generational divides, and politics in the United States and how the same needs that affect separate racial communities are perceived and interpreted differently.

The speech is quoted, in part, below.

Mr. Obama addressed race relations in America by drawing from his own family's history:

186

"I am the son of a black man from Kenya and a white woman from Kansas.

I was raised with the help of a white grandfather who survived a Depression to serve in Patton's Army during World War II and a white grandmother who worked on a bomber assembly line at Fort Leavenworth while he was overseas.

I've gone to some of the best schools in America and lived in one of the world's poorest nations. I am married to a black American who carries within her the blood of slaves and slave-owners - an inheritance we pass on to our two precious daughters.

I have brothers, sisters, nieces, nephews, uncles and cousins, of every race and every hue, scattered across three continents, and for as long as I live, I will never forget that in no other country on Earth is my story even possible.

It's a story that hasn't made me the most conventional candidate.

But it is a story that has seared into my genetic makeup the idea that this nation is more than the sum of its parts - that out of many, we are truly one.......On one end of the spectrum, we've heard the implication that my candidacy is somehow an exercise in affirmative action;

that it's based solely on the desire of wide-eyed liberals to purchase racial reconciliation on the cheap.

Breaking the Myth of Separation and the Deepening Evangelical Division in American Politics

On the other end, we've heard my former pastor, Reverend Jeremiah Wright, use incendiary language to express views that have the potential not only to widen the racial divide, but views that denigrate both the greatness and the goodness of our nation; that rightly offend white and black alike."

His speech also addressed how the quest for Biblical liberation by Reverend Jeremiah Wright can mean different things even within Christian circles:

"I have already condemned, in unequivocal terms, the statements of Reverend Wright that have caused such controversy.

For some, nagging questions remain.

Did I know him to be an occasionally fierce critic of American domestic and foreign policy?

Of course.

Did I ever hear him make remarks that could be considered controversial while I sat in church?

Yes. Did I strongly disagree with many of his political views?

Absolutely - just as I'm sure many of you have heard remarks from your pastors, priests, or rabbis with which you strongly disagreed.

But the remarks that have caused this recent firestorm weren't simply controversial.

They weren't simply a religious leader's effort to speak out against perceived injustice.

Instead, they expressed a profoundly distorted view of this country - a view that sees white racism as endemic, and that elevates what is wrong with America above all that we know is right with America;

A view that sees the conflicts in the Middle East as rooted primarily in the actions of stalwart allies like Israel, instead of emanating from the perverse and hateful ideologies of radical Islam.

As such, Reverend Wright's comments were not only wrong but divisive, divisive at a time when we need unity; racially charged at a time when we need to come together to solve a set of monumental problems - two wars, a terrorist threat, a falling economy, a chronic health care crisis and potentially devastating climate change; problems that are neither black or white or Latino or Asian, but rather problems that confront us all.

Given my background, my politics, and my professed values and ideals, there will no doubt be those for whom my statements of condemnation are not enough.

Why associate myself with Reverend Wright in the first place, they may ask?

Why not join another church?

And I confess that if all that I knew of Reverend Wright were the snippets of those sermons that have run in an endless loop on the television and YouTube, or if Trinity United Church of Christ conformed to the caricatures being peddled by some commentators, there is no doubt that I would react in much the same way

But the truth is, that isn't all that I know of the man. The man I met more than twenty years ago is a man who helped introduce me to my Christian faith, a man who spoke to me about our obligations to love one another; to care for the sick and lift up the poor.

He is a man who served his country as a U.S. Marine; who has studied and lectured at some of the finest universities and seminaries in the country, and who for over thirty years led a church that serves the community by doing God's work here on Earth - by housing the homeless, ministering to the needy, providing day care services and scholarships and prison ministries, and reaching out to those suffering from HIV/AIDS…..

In my first book, 'Dreams From My Father', I described the experience of my first service at Trinity:

'People began to shout, to rise from their seats and clap and cry out, a forceful wind carrying the reverend's voice up into the rafters....And in that single note - hope! - I heard something else; at the foot of that cross, inside the thousands of churches across the city, I imagined the stories of ordinary black people merging with the stories of David and Goliath, Moses and Pharaoh, the Christians in the lion's den, Ezekiel's field of dry bones.

Those stories - of survival, and freedom, and hope - became our story, my story; the blood that had spilled was our blood, the tears our tears; until this black church, on this bright day, seemed once more a vessel carrying the story of a people into future generations and into a larger world.

Our trials and triumphs became at once unique and universal, black and more than black; in chronicling our journey, the stories and songs gave us a means to reclaim memories that we didn't need to feel shame about...memories that all people might study and cherish - and with which we could start to rebuild.'

That has been my experience at Trinity. Like other predominantly black churches across the country, Trinity embodies the black community in its entirety - the doctor and the welfare mom, the model student, and the former gang-banger.

Like other black churches, Trinity's services are full of raucous laughter and sometimes-bawdy humor.

They are full of dancing, clapping, screaming and shouting that may seem jarring to the untrained ear. The church contains in full the kindness and cruelty, the fierce intelligence and the shocking ignorance, the struggles and successes, the love and yes, the bitterness and bias that make up the black experience in America.

And this helps explain, perhaps, my relationship with Reverend Wright. As imperfect as he may be, he has been like family to me.

He strengthened my faith, officiated my wedding, and baptized my children.

Not once in my conversations with him have I heard him talk about any ethnic group in derogatory terms, or treat whites with whom he interacted with anything but courtesy and respect.

He contains within him the contradictions - the good and the bad - of the community that he has served diligently for so many years.

I can no more disown him than I can disown the black community.

I can no more disown him than I can my white grandmother - a woman who helped raise me, a woman who sacrificed again and again for me, a woman who loves me as much as she loves anything in this world, but a woman who once confessed her fear of black men who passed by her on the street, and who on more than one occasion has uttered racial or ethnic stereotypes that made me cringe.

These people are a part of me. And they are a part of America, this country that I love."

Mr. Obama also tackled the root of the race complexities in America:

"Some will see this as an attempt to justify or excuse comments that are simply inexcusable. I can assure you it is not.

I suppose the politically safe thing would be to move on from this episode and just hope that it fades into the woodwork.

We can dismiss Reverend Wright as a crank or a demagogue, just as some have dismissed Geraldine

Ferraro, in the aftermath of her recent statements, as harboring some deep-seated racial bias.

But race is an issue that I believe this nation cannot afford to ignore right now. We would be making the same mistake that Reverend Wright made in his offending sermons about America - to simplify and stereotype and amplify the negative to the point that it distorts reality.

The fact is that the comments that have been made and the issues that have surfaced over the last few weeks reflect the complexities of race in this country that we've never really worked through - a part of our union that we have yet to perfect.

And if we walk away now, if we simply retreat into our respective corners, we will never be able to come together and solve challenges like health care, or education, or the need to find good jobs for every American.

Understanding this reality requires a reminder of how we arrived at this point. As William Faulkner once wrote, "The past isn't dead and buried. In fact, it isn't even past." We do not need to recite here the history of racial injustice in this country.

But we do need to remind ourselves that so many of the disparities that exist in the African-American community today can be directly traced to inequalities passed on from an earlier generation that suffered under the brutal legacy of slavery and Jim Crow.

Segregated schools were, and are, inferior schools; we still haven't fixed them, fifty years after Brown v. Board of Education, and the inferior education they provided, then and now, helps explain the pervasive achievement gap between today's black and white students.

Legalized discrimination - where blacks were prevented, often through violence, from owning property, or loans were not granted to African-American business owners, or black homeowners could not access FHA mortgages, or blacks were excluded from unions, or the police force, or fire departments - meant that black families could not amass any meaningful wealth to bequeath to future generations.

That history helps explain the wealth and income gap between black and white, and the concentrated pockets of poverty that persists in so many of today's urban and rural communities.

A lack of economic opportunity among black men, and the shame and frustration that came from not being able to provide for one's family, contributed to the erosion of black families - a problem that welfare policies for many years may have worsened.

And the lack of basic services in so many urban black neighborhoods - parks for kids to play in, police walking the beat, regular garbage pick-up and building code enforcement - all helped create a cycle of violence, blight and neglect that continue to haunt us.

This is the reality in which Reverend Wright and other African-Americans of his generation grew up.

They came of age in the late fifties and early sixties, a time when segregation was still the law of the land and opportunity was systematically constricted.

What's remarkable is not how many failed in the face of discrimination, but rather how many men and women overcame the odds; how many were able to make a way out of no way for those like me who would come after them.

But for all those who scratched and clawed their way to get a piece of the American Dream, there were many who didn't make it - those who were ultimately defeated, in one way or another, by discrimination.

That legacy of defeat was passed on to future generations - those young men and increasingly young women who we see standing on street corners or languishing in our prisons, without hope or prospects for the future.

Even for those blacks who did make it, questions of race, and racism, continue to define their worldview in fundamental ways.

For the men and women of Reverend Wright's generation, the memories of humiliation and doubt and fear have not gone away; nor has the anger and the bitterness of those years.

That anger may not get expressed in public, in front of white co-workers or white friends. But it does find voice in the barbershop or around the kitchen table.

At times, that anger is exploited by politicians, to gin up votes along racial lines, or to make up for a politician's own failings.

And occasionally it finds voice in the church on Sunday morning, in the pulpit and in the pews.

The fact that so many people are surprised to hear that anger in some of Reverend Wright's sermons simply reminds us of the old truism that the most segregated hour in American life occurs on Sunday morning.

That anger is not always productive; indeed, all too often it distracts attention from solving real problems; it keeps us from squarely facing our own complicity in our condition, and prevents the African-American community from forging the alliances it needs to bring about real change.

But the anger is real; it is powerful; and to simply wish it away, to condemn it without understanding its roots, only serves to widen the chasm of misunderstanding that exists between the races.

In fact, a similar anger exists within segments of the white community.

Most working- and middle-class white Americans don't feel that they have been particularly privileged by their race.

Their experience is the immigrant experience - as far as they're concerned, no one's handed them anything, they've built it from scratch.

They've worked hard all their lives, many times only to see their jobs shipped overseas or their pension dumped after a lifetime of labor.

They are anxious about their futures, and feel their dreams slipping away; in an era of stagnant wages and global competition, opportunity comes to be seen as a zero-sum game, in which your dreams come at my expense.

So when they are told to bus their children to a school across town; when they hear that an African American is getting an advantage in landing a good job or a spot in a good college because of an injustice that they themselves never committed; when they're told that their fears about crime in urban neighborhoods are somehow prejudiced, resentment builds over time.

Like the anger within the black community, these resentments aren't always expressed in polite company.

But they have helped shape the political landscape for at least a generation. Anger over welfare and affirmative action helped forge the Reagan Coalition.

Politicians routinely exploited fears of crime for their own electoral ends.

Talk show hosts and conservative commentators built entire careers unmasking bogus claims of racism while dismissing legitimate discussions of racial injustice and inequality as mere political correctness or reverse racism.

Breaking the Myth of Separation and the Deepening Evangelical Division in American Politics

Just as black anger often proved counterproductive, so have these white resentments distracted attention from the real culprits of the middle class squeeze - a corporate culture rife with inside dealing, questionable accounting practices, and short-term greed; a Washington dominated by lobbyists and special interests; economic policies that favor the few over the many.

And yet, to wish away the resentments of white Americans, to label them as misguided or even racist, without recognizing they are grounded in legitimate concerns - this too widens the racial divide, and blocks the path to understanding.

This is where we are right now. It's a racial stalemate we've been stuck in for years.

Contrary to the claims of some of my critics, black and white, I have never been so naïve as to believe that we can get beyond our racial divisions in a single election cycle, or with a single candidacy - particularly a candidacy as imperfect as my own."

Mr. Obama also dealt with the possibility of better racial relations in America, moving forward:

"But I have asserted a firm conviction - a conviction rooted in my faith in God and my faith in the American people - that working together we can move beyond some of our old racial wounds, and that in fact, we have no choice is we are to continue on the path of a more perfect union.

For the African-American community, that path means embracing the burdens of our past without becoming victims of our past.

It means continuing to insist on a full measure of justice in every aspect of American life.

But it also means binding our particular grievances - for better healthcare, and better schools, and better jobs - to the larger aspirations of all Americans -- the white woman struggling to break the glass ceiling, the white man whose been laid off, the immigrant trying to feed his family.

And it means taking full responsibility for own lives - by demanding more from our fathers, and spending more time with our children, and reading to them, and teaching them that while they may face challenges and discrimination in their own lives, they must never succumb to despair or cynicism; they must always believe that they can write their own destiny.

Ironically, this quintessentially American - and yes, conservative - notion of self-help found frequent expression in Reverend Wright's sermons.

But what my former pastor too often failed to understand is that embarking on a program of self-help also requires a belief that society can change.

The profound mistake of Reverend Wright's sermons is not that he spoke about racism in our society.

It's that he spoke as if our society was static; as if no progress has been made; as if this country - a country that has made it possible for one of his own members to run for the highest office in the land and build a coalition of white and black;

Latino and Asian, rich and poor, young and old -- is still irrevocably bound to a tragic past.

But what we know -- what we have seen - is that America can change. That is true genius of this nation. What we have already achieved gives us hope - the audacity to hope - for what we can and must achieve tomorrow.

In the white community, the path to a more perfect union means acknowledging that what ails the African-American community does not just exist in the minds of black people; that the legacy of discrimination - and current incidents of discrimination, while less overt than in the past - are real and must be addressed.

 Not just with words, but with deeds - by investing in our schools and our communities; by enforcing our civil rights laws and ensuring fairness in our criminal justice system; by providing this generation with ladders of opportunity that were unavailable for previous generations.

It requires all Americans to realize that your dreams do not have to come at the expense of my dreams; that investing in the health, welfare, and education of black and brown and white children will ultimately help all of America prosper.

In the end, then, what is called for is nothing more, and nothing less, than what all the world's great religions demand - that we do unto others as we would have them do unto us. Let us be our brother's keeper, Scripture tells us.

Let us be our sister's keeper. Let us find that common stake we all have in one another, and let our politics reflect that spirit as well.

For we have a choice in this country. We can accept a politics that breeds division, and conflict, and cynicism.

We can tackle race only as spectacle - as we did in the OJ trial - or in the wake of tragedy, as we did in the aftermath of Katrina - or as fodder for the nightly news.

We can play Reverend Wright's sermons on every channel, every day and talk about them from now until the election, and make the only question in this campaign whether or not the American people think that I somehow believe or sympathize with his most offensive words.

We can pounce on some gaffe by a Hillary supporter as evidence that she's playing the race card, or we can speculate on whether white men will all flock to John McCain in the general election regardless of his policies" Mr. Obama remarked.

Then Senator Obama eventually withdrew his membership from the Trinity United Church in Christ.

References

The political and historical discussions in "God and Government" are based on data drawn almost entirely from publicly available sources, including: Websites, publications of government statistical agencies, and from contemporary and historical books.

Introduction:

Adam Philips, "Bishop TD Jakes, Evolved and Evolving on LGBT Issues", posted on 08/05/2015 04:42 pm ET | Updated Aug 05, 2015, at: http://www.huffingtonpost.com/adam-nicholas-phillips/bishop-td-jakes-is-evolved-and-evolving-on-lgbt-issues_b_7942646.html

 Heather Clark, "T.D. Jakes Comes Out for 'Gay Rights' and 'LGBT Churches,' Says Position is 'Evolving'", posted on August 7, 2015, at: http://christiannews.net/2015/08/07/t-d-jakes-comes-out-for-gay-marriage-and-lgbt-churches-says-position-is-evolving/

Aaron Barksdale, "Bishop T.D. Jakes On The Black Church's Shifting Stance On The LGBT

Community" Bishop T.D. Jakes discusses how the LGBT and black church communities can coexist, posted on 08/04/2015 02:07 pm ET | Updated Aug 12, 2015, at: http://www.huffingtonpost.com/entry/td-jakes-says-the-black-church-and-lgbt-community-can-absolutely-coexist_us_55c0cc80e4b0b23e3ce3ff7a http://www.huffingtonpost.com/entry/td-jakes-says-the-black-church-and-lgbt-community-can-absolutely-coexist_us_55c0cc80e4b0b23e3ce3ff7a

Nicola Menzie, "Bishop T.D. Jakes Says He Has Not 'Evolved' on Homosexuality and Does Not 'Endorse' Gay Marriage"

The Potter's House Pastor Clarifies Positions After Huff Post Live Interview Prompts Confusion Among Some, posted on August 11, 2015|4:24 pm, http://www.christianpost.com/news/bishop-t-d-jakes-says-he-has-not-evolved-on-homosexuality-and-does-not-endorse-gay-marriage-142427/

Read more at: http://www.christianpost.com/news/bishop-t-d-jakes-says-he-has-not-evolved-on-homosexuality-and-does-not-endorse-gay-marriage-142427/#C2xMyYv7PCrVe8ku.99

You are here: Opinion ▸ Watchman on the Wall ▸ Bishop T.D. Jakes 'Shocked' to Read 'Manipulation' of His 'Gay Marriage' Comments

Jennifer LeClaire, "Bishop T.D. Jakes 'Shocked' to Read 'Manipulation' of His 'Gay Marriage' Comments", posted on 8/10/2015 12:05PM EDT, at: http://www.charismanews.com/opinion/watchman-on-the-wall/50956-bishop-t-d-jakes-shocked-to-read-manipulation-of-his-gay-marriage-comments

Chapter 2: THE SHIFT IN RELIGIOUS FREEDOMS IN THE OBAMA ERA

Mark Berman, "Mississippi governor signs law allowing businesses to refuse service to gay people", posted on April 5, 2016, at: https://www.washingtonpost.com/news/post-nation/wp/2016/04/05/mississippi-governor-signs-law-allowing-business-to-refuse-service-to-gay-people/

Emanuella Grinberg, "Obama administration issues guidance on transgender access to school bathrooms", posted on May 13, 2016, at: http://www.cnn.com/2016/05/12/politics/transgender-bathrooms-obama-administration/index.html Jonah Hicap , "Families sue U.S. government for pressuring Illinois school to allow transgender in girls' bathroom" posted on 07 May 2016, http://www.christiantoday.com/article/families.sue.u.s.government.for.pressuring.illinois.school.to.allow.transgender.in.girls.bathroom/85506.htm

Lusaka Times, "I'll not impose Gay Rights on Zambians in Exchange for Donor Aid-President Lungu" posted on July 16, 2019, at: https://www.lusakatimes.com/2019/07/16/ill-not-impose-gay-rights-on-zambians-in-exchange-for-donor-aid-president-lungu/

Defense of Marriage Act, at: https://www.govtrack.us/congress/bills/104/hr3396

Defense of Marriage Act (DOMA), at: http://www.glaad.org/marriage/doma

Windsor V. the United States, at: https://www.aclu.org/cases/lesbian-and-gay-rights/windsor-v-united-states

Windsor V. the United States, at: http://www.supremecourt.gov/opinions/12pdf/12-307_6j37.pdf

ELISABETH BUMILLER, "Bush Says His Party Is Wrong to Oppose Gay Civil Unions", posted on October26, 2004, at:

http://www.nytimes.com/2004/10/26/politics/campaign/bush-says-his-party-is-wrong-to-oppose-gay-civil-unions.html?_r=0

Garance Franke-Ruta, "George W. Bush's Forgotten Gay-Rights History", posted on Jul 8, 2013, at: http://www.theatlantic.com/politics/archive/2013/07

/george-w-bushs-forgotten-gay-rights-history/277567/
Pastor Protection Act Passes Unanimously in House of Representatives, posted on February 11, 2016, at: http://openstates.org/ga/legislators/GAL000364/kev in-tanner/

Inside the first Amendment: "Mitt. Mormons and the Religious test that wasn't" by CHARLES C. HAYNES Gannett, posted on November 12, 2012, at: http://www.statesmanjournal.com/article/20121119/OPINION/311190032/Opinion-Mitt-Mormons-religious-test-wasn-t-?odyssey=nav%7Chead

 Dr. Robert Jeffress, Foxnews.com: "Romney and the disappearing evangelical dilemma" posted on September 19, 2012, at: http://www.foxnews.com/opinion/2012/09/19/mitt-romney-and-disappearing-evangelical-dilemma/

JFACTIVIST: "United States Supreme Court will decide important cases on the rights of persons with disabilities", by David Heymsfeld, posted October 5, 2011, at: http://jfactivist.typepad.com/jfactivist/2011/10/united-states-supreme-court-will-decide-important-cases-on-the-rights-of-persons-with-disabilities.html

Adam Liptak, The New York Times: "Religious Groups Given 'Exception' to Work Bias Law", posted on January 11, 2012, at: http://www.nytimes.com/2012/01/12/us/supreme-court-recognizes-religious-exception-to-job-discrimination-laws.html

United States Conference of Catholic Bishops: "Conscience Protection", at: http://www.usccb.org/issues-and-action/religious-liberty/conscience-protection/

Meghashyam Mali, The Hill's Blog Briefing Room: "NAACP endorses gay marriage as 'civil right'", posted on 05/20/2012, at: http://thehill.com/blogs/blog-briefing-room/news/228463-naacp-endorses-gay-marriage-as-civil-right

CBN News: "Black Churches Denounce NAACP Gay Marriage stance" posted on Tuesday May 22, 2012, at: http://www.cbn.com/cbnnews/us/2012/May/Black-Churches-Denounce-NAACP-Gay-Marriage-Stance/

Foxnews.com: "Romney and the disappearing evangelical dilemma" by Dr. Robert Jeffress, posted on September 19, 2012, at:

http://www.foxnews.com/opinion/2012/09/19/mitt-romney-and-disappearing-evangelical-dilemma/

NCSL: "Defining Marriage: Defense of Marriage Acts and Same-Sex Marriage Laws", at: http://www.ncsl.org/issues-research/human-services/same-sex-marriage-overview.aspx

Josh Lederman, "Trump administration launches global effort to end criminalization of homosexuality" posted on February 19th, 2019, at: https://www.nbcnews.com/politics/national-security/trump-administration-launches-global-effort-end-criminalization-homosexuality-n973081?cid=sm_npd_ms_fb_ma&fbclid=IwAR2e FWvDfzZBopKXgf4v7cEckYtUAG8g4OR7WbEs 6-tQ_yVdBf_W3BF-6bY

BBC News US and Canada: "Hillary Clinton declares 'gay rights are human rights" posted on December 7, 2011 at http://www.bbc.co.uk/news/world-us-canada-16062937

Around the World: "Global Gay Rights, from Marriage to the Death Penalty" By Christiane Amanpour, Mary-Rose Abraham, David Miller & Brad Marxer, posted on January 3, 2013 at http://news.yahoo.com/blogs/around-the-world-abcnews/global-gay-rights-marriage-death-penalty-153355943.html

By TMG Digital, "Tutu's daughter marries in small civil ceremony",
Posted on Jan 02, 2016, at:
http://www.sowetanlive.co.za/news/2016/01/02/tutus-daughter-marries.-in-small-civil-ceremony

The New York Times: "U.S. to Aid Gay Rights Abroad, Obama and Clinton Say" By STEVEN LEE MYERS and HELENE COOPER Published: December 6, 2011 at
http://www.nytimes.com/2011/12/07/world/united-states-to-use-aid-to-promote-gay-rights-abroad.html?pagewanted=all

BBC News US and Canada: "Hillary Clinton declares 'gay rights are human rights" posted on December 7, 2011 at
http://www.bbc.co.uk/news/world-us-canada-16062937

BBC Africa: "Nigerian leaders unite against same-sex marriages" By Jonah Fisher BBC News, Abuja, posted on December 5, 2011 at
http://www.bbc.co.uk/news/world-africa-15992099

JEFFREY GETTLEMAN, "Uganda Anti-Gay Law Struck Down by Court", posted in AUG. 1, 2014, at:

http://www.nytimes.com/2014/08/02/world/africa/u ganda-anti-gay-law-struck-down-by- court.html?_r=0

BBC Africa: "Ghana refuses to grant gays' rights despite aid threat" posted on November 2, 2011 at http://www.bbc.co.uk/news/world-africa-15558769

Jen Kirby, "Taiwan's parliament passes historic same-sex marriage law", posted on May 17th, 2019, at: https:// www.vox.comworld/2019/5/17/18629156/ta iwan- same-sex-marriage-legalization-lgbtq-asia

BBC Asia, "Taiwan voters reject same-sex marriage in referendums", posted on November 25th, 2018, at: https://www.bbc.com/news/world- asia-46329877

Morgan Gstalter, "Brazil's new president removes LGBT concerns from human rights ministry", posted on January 2nd, 2019, at: https://thehill.com/policy/international/human- rights/423594-brazils-new-president-removes-lgbt- concerns-from-human

Mauricio Savarese, AP, "Brazil's Bolsonaro targets indigenous groups, LGBTQ rights on 1st day as president", posted on January 2nd, 2019, at:

https://www.pbs.org/newshour/world/brazils-
bolsonaro-targets-indigenous-groups-lgbtq-rights-
on-1st-day-as-president

Thomas Iglesias Trombetta ,"Why Canadians
Should Pay Attention to Brazil's War on 'Gender
Ideology", posted on February 4th, 2019, at:
https://www.vice.com/en_ca/article/mbzggy/why-
canadians-should-pay-attention-to-brazils-war-on-
gender-
ideology?utm_source=vicefbca&utm_campaign=gl
obal&fbclid=IwAR2yu1bKWCWG-
gjqEubnkXAtMoT0ngunFvAIl0tmthN67cLgtzPkrT
r2gP0

By Liz Fields, "Nuns Are Battling Birth Control
Provision at the US Supreme Court" posted on
March 24, 2016, 9:07 am, at:
https://news.vice.com/article/nuns-are-battling-
birth-control-provision-at-the-us-supreme-court

 Colleen Curry, "How Hobby Lobby Paved the Way
for the Current Rush of Religious Freedom Laws",
posted on March 31, 2015, 4:55 pm, at:
https://news.vice.com/article/how-hobby-lobby-
paved-the-way-for-the-current-rush-of-religious-
freedom-laws

Nina Totenberg, "Birth Control At The Supreme
Court: Does Free Coverage Violate Religious
Freedom?" posted on March 23, 2016, 5:00 AM
ET, at:

http://www.npr.org/2016/03/23/471003272/birth-control-at-the-supreme-court-does-free-coverage-violate-religious-freedom

CHAPTER 3: THE CHRISTIAN RIGHT'S INFLUENCE IN AMERICAN POLITICS

David Jackson, "Donald Trump accepts GOP nomination, says 'I alone can fix' system", posted on July 21st, 2016, at:
https://www.usatoday.com/story/news/politics/elections/2016/07/21/donald-trump-republican-convention-acceptance-speech/87385658/

Yoni Appelbaum, "'I Alone Can Fix It'", posted on July 21st, 2016, at:
https://www.theatlantic.com/politics/archive/2016/07/trump-rnc-speech-alone-fix-it/492557/

Reuters Politics, "Trump says sets measure to punish companies that outsource", posted on October 10th, 2017, at:
https://www.reuters.com/article/us-usa-trump-outsource/trump-says-sets-measure-to-punish-companies-that-outsource-idUSKBN1CF1IF

J. Brian Charles, "Transcript of Donald Trump's economic policy speech to Detroit Economic Club", posted on August 8th, 2016, at:
https://thehill.com/blogs/pundits-blog/campaign/290777-transcript-of-donald-trumps-economic-policy-speech-to-detroit

Philip Bump, "It's hard to imagine a much worse pitch Donald Trump could have made for the black vote", posted on August 20th, 2016, at: https://www.washingtonpost.com/news/the-fix/wp/2016/08/20/its-hard-to-imagine-a-much-worse-pitch-donald-trump-could-have-made-for-the-black-vote/?noredirect=on&utm_term=.1735c8a3a0e8

CHAPTER 4: IDENTITY POLITICS AND THE DEEPENING EVANGELICAL DIVISION

"President Donald J. Trump Stands Up For Religious Freedom In The United States", posted on May 3rd, 2018, at: https://www.whitehouse.gov/briefings-statements/president-donald-j-trump-stands-religious-freedom-united-states/

PBS News Hour, "Trump administration asks Supreme Court to hear transgender military case", posted on November 23rd, 2018, at: https://www.pbs.org/newshour/politics/trump-administration-asks-supreme-court-to-hear-transgender-military-case?fbclid=IwAR3H2XMJCsklTcBGWlc4rsXRe42UH-GqsEbyvcgbMgmAynUAMpuQvo0jYs4Jeremy

Weber, "Billy Graham Center Explains Survey on Evangelical Trump Voters", posted on October 18th, 2018, at: https://www.christianitytoday.com/news/2018/octob

er/evangelicals-trump-2016-election-billy-graham-center-survey.html

Bob Smietana, "What Is an Evangelical? Four Questions Offer New Definition", posted on November 19th, 2015, at: https://www.christianitytoday.com/news/2015/november/what-is-evangelical-new-definition-nae-lifeway-research.html

CNN, "CNN's Anderson Cooper speaks with Jerry Falwell Jr., president of Liberty University about his endorsement of Donald Trump", posted on June 1, 2016, at: https://www.youtube.com/watch?v=G42VEGGmliQ
"Jerry Falwell Jr.: Trump is the Churchillian leader we need", By Jerry Falwell, Jr., posted on June 1st, 2016, at: https://www.washingtonpost.com/opinions/jerry-falwell-jr-trump-is-the-churchillian-leader-we-need/2016/08/19/b1ff79e0-64b1-11e6-be4e-23fc4d4d12b4_story.html?noredirect=on&utm_term=.2a30c78b6807

Mckay Coppins,"God's Plan for Mike Pence: Will the vice president—and the religious right—be rewarded for their embrace of Donald Trump?", posted in the January/February Issue, at: https://www.theatlantic.com/magazine/archive/2018/01/gods-plan-for-mike-pence/546569/?fbclid=IwAR0rA2-

_KAycyho_ST6SkGG15pmFaThSU6gXj-VrXuSdWb-P4KzmYW3yXzQ&utm_campaign=the-atlantic&utm_content=5bf7b3813ed3f00001b426f3_ta&utm_medium=social&utm_source=facebook

The Atlantic, "We've Reached the End of White Christian America", Video, posted on October 13, 2016, at:
https://www.theatlantic.com/video/index/504065/america-post-christianity/?utm_campaign=the-atlantic&utm_medium=social&utm_source=facebook&utm_term=2018-11-16T21%3A43%3A01&utm_content=edit-promo&fbclid=IwAR3mp6WJrMl1XjeFpJYOqsZfn5_G8xa2nCvsPpfowZMMjN8IhxuUHaO--34

PRRI, "Partisan Polarization Dominates Trump Era: Findings from the 2018 American Values Survey", posted on October 29th, 2018, at:
https://www.prri.org/research/partisan-polarization-dominates-trump-era-findings-from-the-2018-american-values-survey/

Carol Kuruvilla, "Evangelical Pastor Claims Trump's Immigration Policies Are Biblical", posted on November 6th, 2018, at:
https://www.huffingtonpost.com/entry/tony-perkins-immigration-bible_us_5be1b756e4b04367a880f4ef?ncid=fcbklnkushpmg00000013&utm_source=politics_fb&utm_campaign=hp_fb_pages&section=politics&utm_medium=facebook&fbclid=IwAR25ZdFGMlXBVoS8

5yXAb9MXXANbqPesysuf52Wtb1ycQgiA7qobw
Ky7b7E

Ed Stetzer, "Fellow evangelicals: stop falling for Trump's anti-immigrant rhetoric", posted on November 6th, 2018, at: https://www.vox.com/policy-and-politics/2018/11/6/18066116/trump-caravan-evangelical-voters

NEW DAY, "Christian Leaders Divided on Border Policy; Roseanne Makes Apology; Sanders Asked to Leave Restaurant. ", Aired June 25, 2018 - Aired 8:30-9a ET, at: http://transcripts.cnn.com/TRANSCRIPTS/1806/25/nday.06.html

The Economist, "Why evangelicals love Donald Trump", print edition, posted May 18th, 2017, at: https://www.economist.com/united-states/2017/05/18/why-evangelicals-love-donald-trump?fsrc=scn/fb/te/bl/ed/lexingtonwhyevangelicalslovedonaldtrump

Sean Illing, "This is why evangelicals love Trump's Israel policy", posted on May 18th, 2018, at: https://www.vox.com/2017/12/12/16761540/jerusalem-israel-embassy-palestinians-trump-evangelicals

Shibley Telhami, "Why is Trump undoing decades of U.S. Policy on Jerusalem?", posted on December 5, 2018, at:

https://www.brookings.edu/blog/markaz/2017/12/05/why-is-trump-about-to-declare-jerusalem-the-capital-of-israel/

Jack Jenkins, "Nobody is laughing at the Religious Left in 2017", posted on December 13th, 2017, at: https://thinkprogress.org/2017-is-the-year-trump-and-the-religious-right-made-the-religious-left-unavoidable-3e89528104b6/

Scott Malone, "'Religious left' emerging as U.S. political force in Trump era", posted on March 17th, 2017, at: https://www.reuters.com/article/us-usa-trump-religion/religious-left-emerging-as-u-s-political-force-in-trump-era-idUSKBN16Y114

Carol Kuruvilla, "Quakers, Rabbis, Imams Protest for Migrants Rights Because 'Love knows No Border'", posted on December 12th, 2018, at: https://www.huffingtonpost.com/entry/interfaith-border-protest-migrants_us_5c112943e4b0ac53717af2ce

Rosey Gray "Trump Defends White-Nationalist Protesters: 'Some Very Fine People on Both Sides'", posted on August 15th, 2017, at: https://www.theatlantic.com/politics/archive/2017/08/trump-defends-white-nationalist-protesters-some-very-fine-people-on-both-sides/537012/

Sarah Pulliam Bailey, "Megachurch pastor resigns from Trump's evangelical council", posted on August 18th, 2017, at

Breaking the Myth of Separation and the Deepening Evangelical Division in American Politics

https://www.washingtonpost.com/news/acts-of-faith/wp/2017/08/18/megachurch-pastor-resigns-from-trumps-evangelical-council/?utm_term=.07306fc4694e

Leonardo Blair, "Evangelical Advisory Board Is 'Photo Op' for Donald Trump, Pastor AR Bernard Says on Exit", posted on August 21st, 2017, at: https://www.christianpost.com/news/evangelical-advisory-board-is-photo-op-for-donald-trump-pastor-ar-bernard-says-on-exit.html

Brandon Showalter, "Pastor AR Bernard Leaves Trump's Evangelical Advisory Board Citing 'Deepening Conflict in Values'", posted on August 19th, 2017, at: https://www.christianpost.com/news/pastor-a-r-bernard-leaves-trumps-evangelical-advisory-board-citing-deepening-conflict-in-values.html

Farah Meralli, CBC News, "Local Christian leaders don't want evangelist Franklin Graham speaking in Vancouver", posted on February 20, 2017, at: https://www.cbc.ca/news/canada/british-columbia/leaders-launch-petition-against-franklin-graham-1.3991375

Flyn Ritchie, "Critics look forward to Festival of Hope – without Franklin Graham", posted on February 16th, 2017, at: https://churchforvancouver.ca/critics-look-forward-to-festival-of-hope-without-franklin-graham/

Breaking the Myth of Separation and the Deepening Evangelical Division in American Politics

Bob Allen, "Pastors oppose Franklin Graham crusade in Canada", posted on September 2nd, 2016, at: https://baptistnews.com/article/pastors-oppose-franklin-graham-crusade-in-canada/#.XFyt0vx7k1g

Franklin Graham Facebook page, posted on July 17th, 2017, at : https://www.facebook.com/FranklinGraham/posts/9 67305353325646

Franklin Graham's page, posted on January 31st, 2017, at: https://www.facebook.com/FranklinGraham/posts/1 394064260649751

Franklin Graham, "Putin's Olympic Controversy", posted on February 28th, 2014, at: https://billygraham.org/decision-magazine/march-%202014/putins-olympic-%20controversy/

Emma Green, "Franklin Graham Is the Evangelical Id", posted on May 21st, 2017, at: https://www.theatlantic.com/politics/archive/2017/0 5/franklin-graham/527013/

ACLU-Washington, "Time Line of the Travel Ban", at: https://www.aclu-wa.org/pages/timeline-muslim-ban

Catherine E Soichet and Gary Tuchman, CNN, "Chattanooga shooting: 4 Marines killed, a dead suspect and questions of motive", posted on July 17, 2017 at:
https://www.cnn.com/2015/07/16/us/tennessee-naval-reserve-shooting/index.html

Mythili Sampathkumar, "Trump travel ban: What is the controversial immigration measure given green light by Supreme Court ruling", posted on June 27th, 2018, at:
https://www.independent.co.uk/news/world/americas/us-politics/travel-ban-trump-supreme-court-what-is-muslim-countries-a8418361.html

CHAPTER 5: THE BIBLICAL STRUCTURES OF GOVERNMENT
Gary DeMar, God and Government, Paperback Volume1, (American vision, second revised version 1992) Chapters 1 and 2

CHAPTER 6: THE BIBLICAL ROLES OF STATE GOVERNMENT

Gary DeMar, God and Government, Paperback Volume1, (American vision, second revised version 1992), Chapters 3, 4 and 5

CHAPTER 7: POLITICS ABHORS A VACUUM

Our Daily Bread: "Nature abhors a vacuum" by Julie Ackerman Link posted on January 21, 2011 at http://odb.org/2011/01/21/nature-abhors-a-vacuum/

American Federalist Journal: "Abraham Lincoln"
Selected Quotes at
http://www.federalistjournal.com/ref/quotes1.php

South African History online, The Dutch Reformed
Church, at:
http://www.sahistory.org.za/article/dutch-reformed-
church-south-african-history-online

Re: QUEST ISUES, "Prejudice and Discrimination"
at
http://www.request.org.uk/issues/topics/prejudice/pr
ejudice09.htm

Truth and Reconciliation Commission Final Report,
Volume 4 Chapter 3

Dutch Reformed Church of South Africa at
http://www.philtar.ac.uk/encyclopedia/christ/cep/dr
csa.html

John Calvin Biography at:
http://christianity.about.com/od/presbyteriandenomi
nation/a/John-Calvin.htm

South African History Online: "Dutch Reformed
Church" at
http://www.sahistory.org.za/article/dutch-reformed-
church-south-african-history-online

South Africa, "Religion and Apartheid" at
http://www.photius.com/countries/south_africa/soci
ety/south_africa_society_religion_and_aparthe~245
1.html

Richard Downes, Dispatches: Africa, BBC News,
posted on November 19, 1997 at
http://news.bbc.co.uk/2/hi/despatches/africa/33032.s
tm

South Africa, "overcoming Apartheid, Building
Democracy" at
http://overcomingapartheid.msu.edu/sidebar.php?id
=8

Etymology: "Democracy in Greek" at
http://en.wikipedia.org/wiki/Democracy

The History Place: "Abraham Lincoln: The
Gettysburg Address" at
http://www.historyplace.com/speeches/gettysburg.h
tm

Chapter 9: THE SEPARATION OF CHURCH
AND STATE

"Our founding fathers were not Christians", at:
http://www.freethought.mbdojo.com/foundingfather
s.html

Associated Press, posted on July 4, 2015, "What

you should know about forgotten founding father John Jay", at:
http://www.pbs.org/newshour/rundown/forgotten-founding-father/

John Jay – Quote, at:
http://www.redbubble.com/people/cometman/writing/2153433-john-jay-quote-of-the-day

Wall builders, "John Jay- 1816", at:
http://www.wallbuilders.com/libissuesarticles.asp?id=64

US Treasury Department, "History of 'In God We Trust", at:
https://www.treasury.gov/about/education/Pages/in-god-we-trust.aspx

Simon Brown, ""Coining Controversy" During The Civil War, Conservative Clergy And Their Political Allies Added 'In God We Trust' To American Coins", posted in June 2013, at:

https://www.au.org/church-state/june-2013-church-state/featured/coining-controversy

BBC News: "Why the Pilgrim Fathers left England" posted on Sunday June 18, 1998 at
http://news.bbc.co.uk/2/hi/uk_news/47688.stm

The Declaration of Independence and the Constitution of the United States of America: Amendment 1 "Freedom of Religion, Press and

Expression." Ratified on 12/15/1791. Page 37. (Tribeca Books)

All about History: "Separation of Church and State" at http://www.allabouthistory.org/separation-of-church-and-state.htm

The Declaration of Independence and the Constitution of the United States of America: "The unanimous Declaration of the thirteen United States of America" In Congress, July 4, 1776. Page 55. (Tribeca Books)

America's Founding Fathers: "Frame of the government of Pennsylvania-William Penn" at http://americasfoundingfathers.com/index.php/frame-of-government-of-pennsylvania-1682

Gary DeMar, "Ruler of nations", at: http://www.garynorth.com/freebooks/docs/pdf/ruler_of_the_nations.pdf

CHAPTER 10: BOTTOM-UP HIERARCHY OF GOVERNMENT
http://www.garynorth.com/freebooks/docs/pdf/ruler_of_the_nations.pdf

The New world order: http://www.biblebelievers.org.au/nv2.htm

Michael Snyder, "Did the United Nations Just Introduce a New World Order?"

Posted on 9/30/2015, at:
http://www.charismanews.com/opinion/52333-did-the-united-nations-just-introduce-a-new-world-order

"What is the New World Order?" at:
http://www.gotquestions.org/new-world-order.html

CHAPTER 11: GOD'S JUDGMENT OF NATIONS

Gary DeMar, "Ruler of nations", at:
http://www.garynorth.com/freebooks/docs/pdf/ruler of the nations.pdf

CHAPTER 12: MORAL CONSIENCE GOVERNS A NATION 'S CORE VALUES

The Beheading of John the Baptist,
www.christianity.com
CHAPTER 13: RACE, CHURCH, AND POLITICS IN THE UNITED STATES

Wesleyan Wisdom: James had it right-"Faith without Works is dead", by Donald W. Hynes, posted on June 12, 2012, at:
http://www.unitedmethodistreporter.com/2012/06/wesleyan-wisdom-james-had-it-right-faith-without-works-is-dead/

Sunday morning, our country's "most segregated hour", Unites people in Oakland, by Yirmeyah

Beckles and Julia Marshall, posted on February 15, 2012, at:
http://oaklandnorth.net/2012/02/15/sunday-morning-our-countrys-most-segregated-hour-unites-people-in-oakland/

"Why Sunday morning remains America's most segregated hour" posted on October 6th, 2010 at:
http://religion.blogs.cnn.com/2010/10/06/why-sunday-morning-remains-americas-most-segregated-hour/

Reverend Jeremiah Wright's famous quotes at
http://bumpshack.com/2008/03/18/pastor-jeremiah-wright-controversy-quotes/

Obama Race Speech, posted on November 17, 2008 at:
http://www.huffingtonpost.com/2008/03/18/obama-race-speech-read-th_n_92077.html

227

*Breaking the Myth of Separation and the Deepening Evangelical
Division in American Politics*

CPSIA information can be obtained
at www.ICGtesting.com
Printed in the USA
BVHW081516070521
606759BV00009B/1613